Packing to Die

The Suitcase Between Your Ears

George A. Ure
Texas, USA
June 2021

Table of Contents:

Reader Notes, Citation Conventions

This is a book about Death, dying, dying well, postponing it, work plans to do it right, and some field reports from people who have gone head-to-head with the logistical nightmare of death.

In previous books, I have included literally *hundreds* of footnotes.

Not in this one.

The reasons are two-fold: First, this document is published first (as my books are) for my *Peoplenomics.com* newsletter subscribers. Footnotes, even in professional-grade software, doesn't fit mixed media (Amazon *Kindle*, native .HTML, and WordPress) nicely.

Second reason is "return on time invested." If there's something I offer in the book, simply Google it. You should be able to find it quickly. That's a much better approach and helps keep the online cost of this book low.

Third reason? I'm a writer, author, software design geek, management sort. I'm not trying to puff up my resume for some "next gig."

As you're about to discover, there is a kind of resume padding for death, but let's keep that for the chapter on the *After-Life Film School*.

That one matters.

Who You? Who Me? Why This?

Who me first, I guess?

Old 70-something adventurer living in the Outback of East Texas who has spent a lifetime trying to live *somewhat* as God/Nature/Universe intended.

A Life of Adventure? You bet! Traveling, skill-building, academic studies, creating, writing, eating, farming, flying, ham radio, inventing, driving, scuba diving, sailing, cooking, designing…the list is extensive, and it's been a serious kick-in-the ass. Joyriding through Life. It's a Big Buffet and I've been blessed to have gone through the line several times.

Reminds me of a bumper sticker on my friend Jim's car, back when we were both liveaboard sailors in Seattle on offshore capable boats. Sticker read:

"I spent all my money on wine, women, and sailboats. The rest I wasted."

If you want my resume, check the UrbanSurvival.com or Peoplenomics.com websites. Jim's? His graphics code is in many great video games.

So, what are my main credentials for writing this book?

- I've been a reporter. Reporting on Death was really lousy – a spiritual bummer. But we all gotta go...

- I've made many (seems like ALL) of the classic mistakes in Life, too: Divorce, weight gain, not enough exercise, should have made more money….
- But mainly I'm now sneaking up on OLD.
- Which, coupled with a cynical bad attitude, uniquely qualifies me to start Packing to Die.

Most "things" – money, property, tangibles – won't leave with us when *you and I "exit, stage right."* What endures? Feelings, Memories, Learning, Attitudes, Core Beliefs, Mental Pictures, and Mental Video Clips, and so much more. Might not be much use for recipes, though.

Ever wonder how much conscious attention or forethought is paid to such things? Truth is *damn little.* Denial runs off the chickens. The chickens fund the Death Industries.

Looking at the problem of "dying" I didn't see a useful book. One that would "cover the waterfront" and really offer useful tips. How to look at life, how to "pack between the ears" – how to avoid it as long as possible, and how to set it up so everyone left alive gets maximum benefit.

Young people have no business writing about Death. You need to have stared it down a few times. Sure, the kids *may* encounter it – *in passing,* so to speak - when some near and dear takes the final exit, or whatever. But until you size up the heirs, the cost of dying *fast* versus very *slowly*…heroic measures or not, and other such decisions? Naw. Kids think they know more than the grown-ups. But that never changes, does it? They're almost universally unqualified to speak on topic.

Then? Once you go through the Big Changes as a result of Aging - sex drive, finances, medical issues, wrinkles, and all that – *all foreign to the kids* – Dying is just a rumor. A *Youtube* of someone else. Except this time, it's not.

Once you hit *at least* 70, then *maybe* you can throw in your two-bits worth; not before, though.

This book will take you across the Frontiers of Death.

We will ponder whether this is all a computer simulation; maybe it's an arty way for consciousness to explore the Universe. We'll consider our Greater Purpose in Life. I'll be proposing that Life is like a Film School. Life is your "Project."

From these core concepts, we'll evolve into soaking more Personal Power from the Universe to repurpose ourselves and redirect new energy for our own uses. Work on personality traits that can aid us personally in Death avoidance.

After this pile of research, Project Management and metrics are applied to Death and Dying. Then some *Peoplenomics.com* readers share useful key insights into the ugly financial burdens of dying.

Sure, along the way we'll consider "plugging the dike" with exercise, activity, purposes, and supplements. Using all of these, along with good genetics luck, you have very good odds of getting to the Century mark. Some of my personal experiments in low level laser light therapy might even get you further, or at least keep the hair dark and postpone dementia.

But in the end, there's a long stretch of track between spiritual hobo destinations. Least we can do is honor it with mental screen snags to take for showing in the next hobo jungle we land in.

This last shows up in "the literature" as the Life Review.

1.   Basics and a Reader Warning

We ought to get some things straight between us right now.

First: This book is not a sales piece for any particular point of view, religion, philosophy, science, creed, political party, gender, national origin, currency, or any of that. Like booze, Life's a matter of personal taste. Depending, of course, what kind of "high" you're after and what day (and time) it is.

Since you're an independent cuss, you already realize most of your top-of-mind "beliefs" are based on "signal noise" in your environment such as home, work, or school. Repeat a noise often enough and it becomes part of us. Pavlov 101. (Ding!) Media of any kind keeps people stupid to the extent every thought is not inspected and challenged. The busier we get, the less time for introspection and critical thought.

Like social media, that's a big mistake.

Groups of humans "school-up like fish" physically (and on the Internet) to assign labels to causes. Some are right; many are wrong. Each *Labeling Agency* claims their *cause* to be a *Very Big Deal* of in everyday Life. This is mostly bullshit. Equality is evident throughout Nature. All souls weigh the same, regardless of color.

Big shocker here for the pseudo-Woke: *Climate Change* is <u>not</u> the biggest thing in Life. *Gender-selling* <u>is not, either</u>. *Higher Taxes* <u>don't matter</u> in the long run.

In the very short-term, the ONLY important thing in your life at any instant is that you can take *one more* breath. If you don't? The ride's over. Climate, gender-peddling, taxes, cryptos, rigged voting machines? None of it matters in the next minute. Breathing, on the other hand, absolutely, totally, and most assuredly DOES matter.   Which is useful to keep in mind why? Because, like I said…

This is a book about Death and Dying.

Except for competing religionist's *claims*, there is little *scientific* basis to expect a "pass" or "Get Out of Death Free" card at your own End.

Some religionists peddle variants of these. Offering spirit guides of one sort, or another. Certainly, these are welcome. But if there's a guarantee, why do they want 10% of your paycheck in Life? Hard questions. Value judgements multiply.
Let's not change religions, become atheists, or stop tithing, though. Instead, let's <u>follow the data</u> to some useful conclusions. Religions do house useful data sets.

If you're not comfortable (yet) confronting the topic of Death, there's still time to set this book aside. Wait a few years. Go hide under the bed and pretend that you're immortal. Death will come for you anyway. With luck, when events force you to re-examine your *self-delusions* about end of Life, you can come back to this book later. Bring facts when you come, though. Bad news is we're very much data based.

Wait! There's further bad news?

Uh-huh. Even if you happen to be asleep when Death comes around, it WILL nevertheless come for you anyway. You can't "sleep though it" because if you try, you don't wake up. Then you've lost the chance to "make right." You can't send back reliable additional notes to your Executor(s).

You're not immortal in the *here and now*. Mortality comes with each and every visit to the "Earthly Plane of Existence." Like the early *Disneyland* "E" ticket rides (the best ones!) you get on at one end, and off at the other. No feeding back to the people in line waiting to get on. Joy of Walt Disney's notion of "hiding the weenie" in Imagineer terms.

Fortunately, there is a ton of good news about Death and Dying (sounds paradoxical, though, don't it?) which we'll get into as the facts and data piles are laid out. Not to be redundant here, but…

Point #1: You ARE going to Die

Get this through your noggin. Embrace it: You ARE going to die. *You are in a once-only position to get this one right.*

"You said there was some 'good news' in Dying?"

The secret smart adrenaline junkies like me (or my son) already know: *"It's better to have really LIVED once, than not have really Lived at all!"*

See, once you've looked Death 'bang in the eye' a few times (and remembered to *spit*) what remains of Life becomes incredibly *deeper* and more *vibrant*. The feeling of *"extreme aliveness"* never leaves. When it weakens, there's always a new relationship, a Porsche with a 5-speed, an aircraft, racing boat, ripcord, a good new deed to do randomly, or a marathon waiting to refresh that ZEST for Life.

People who *don't* embrace their own death at some emotional levels are free to remain accomplished liars, cheats, and poseurs. Frauds missing the spicy toppings available. It's OK. They *will* get *theirs* in the end.

A long dead DJ and racecar driver I worked with by the name of Art looked me directly in the eye when we met for the first time in the hallway of a radio station (KMPS in Seattle, about 1975, or so). *"You have it."*

"I have What?"

"The Look. You see it in the eyes of racecar drivers, pilots - you fly, right? – and so do all adventurers who've been To the Edge."

Since he pointed it out, I've been looking for it – and seeing it in *some* - ever since. People *vitally alive. Pushing limits, going to the edges and margins to explore.* Art was extraordinarily perceptive that way. Ever since, looking people in the eye, I look for the telltale (hard to describe) that gives away what's 'special' about those who have been "to the Edge." They don't avert their eyes, they aren't sheep. And above all, they have conquered fear.

Life, you've gotta understand, is like a buffet line. A damn near unlimited assortment of experiences to sample and savor.

If your life isn't feeling "right" yet, it's probably because so many people go through the line taking only one item. Mostly out of habit. You really ought to knock that shit off. There's a whole Banquet of Life. You're a fool to miss out.

The full *experience* of "the Banquet" isn't from eating 47-ounces of prime rib. Instead think in terms of balance. Start with 6-ounces of prime rib, an 8-ounce lobster tail, a twice-baked stuffed potato. Maybe before that a warmup of 3-ounces of Scotch & water. Ginormous Dungeness crab cocktail. Followed by a perfectly dressed salad, and a half-hour of great conversation to prepare the mind and pallet for the main courses. Cherries Jubilee flambé for dessert?

You don't have to sample Life. You can keep eating the oatmeal of daily boring. But you can do that alone. And there may not be "something in your eye" that reveals you really know how to Live. You'll have missed the point of Life.

Part of embracing Death is self-criticism. Which can be harsh. But, done right, criticism opens the doors to changing any personal behaviors you want during Life. Only while it's "still playing" in the mind and heart - of <u>you</u>.

Point #2: You Can Plan for Dying

Plan to die? How utterly morbid, right? I mean, seriously? People plan to get up tomorrow and go to work, to the store, to the gym, on a cruise this fall…all kinds of planned activities. Death planning isn't something people are anxious to list. But, why should dying be any different? You can "pack for it." Besides, not like it's *optional*, or anything.

We will attack the topic on several levels. The first – and frankly pretty damn interesting part – is about the dying process. We have so much "baggage" around the whole "getting Dead thing" it's shocking there aren't more commonsense books about it. Most come with religious strings attached, though.

As you know, people don't want to *face* the problem head-on. So, if a group comes along offering *salvation* it might work on you. So, you can "pretend" you're not dying like everyone else. This is one reason people line up to give money to religions. Gimme a chorus of *Stairway to Heaven*, while we're at it.

A later part of this book is dreadfully close to being a *workbook*. Yeah, I hate four-letter words like "work" myself. Checklist, then.

We have a lot of tasks to address if we're going to "Leave Life In Style." Failing to do so, however, can really trash your "*Life flashed before your eyes*" Life replay film (we'll get to this in a later chapter) when the Lights Go Out.

Some "Pre-Noodles" then?

If you have assets, how do you decide how to divvy those up? One reason to have a spouse is to kick the "When I Die" tasks onto someone else's plate. Not very loving of you. Still, *"thems that live longest, call the tune"* in Wills and property, and such.

There's the physical paring down of Earthly goods, too.

Funny story here: I figured out one day that the reason I had stacked up *so many projects around me* was to be "too busy to die!" As a courtesy, I'm dialing it back now. Too much work for survivors. Even a confirmed geek doesn't need one of every kind of welder (except laser, and I'm shopping for one of those), 21 complete ham radio stations, 30 acres of land, a garden, woodshop, metal shop, 3D printer farm and CNC machines. In close proximity with exotic tools, that I haven't spent enough time with…yet. Like the mortising machine that drills "square holes" on command.

You get the idea: Someone's got to clean house. Figure if I do it, I can buy a case or two of good Scotch to sample while waiting for the exit call. If you don't do your own pare-down, someone else may just back up a dump truck and *whoosh!* Lost value. Money that could have gone to survivors. Following? We come in with nothing and leave with nothing PHYSICAL. Whole Game of Life ends upstairs and behind the eyes, between the ears.

Wills are a given. But so is the "Dead Letter" – a concept I came up with years back when there was an inkling "Ever After" might actually show up some day. Rumors I'd Die had persisted for a couple of decades. But when Pappy left from Alzheimer's at 82, and Mom followed at 93, the rumors about Death were turning into a tough customer to deny.

I decided it was time to armor up.

There is also a financial planning part of this book. Some of it will make your hair stand on end.   Not to frighten you, but one of our long-time reader's experiences will sober you right up. Much to be learned from that. Along with some supernatural events from the nursing home circuit.

With this brief survey of "The Being Dead Problem" as a tasking document, let's adjust the reading specification just a bit and begin with a nice, cheerfully chapter titled….

2. Death: Cultural Terrorism 101

Life and Death are the Dance between Dualism and Unity.

Life (when alive) is about Duality. Good/bad. Up/down, right/left, black/white, green/red, many/few, and our favorite: Sense/Nonsense.

Death (the Afterlife) is about Unity: Whole. Being. One. Forever, Eternity, and so forth.

The big fuzzy secret in religions is the Trinity is Good/Bad/One. Up/Down/One. Without the *Duality* of Life, the *Unity* of Death and Immortality cannot exist. Unity (in a Divine Comedy of Language) cannot exist except as a *comparison* to something *Else*. Something in pieces. Sort of like the modern United States which isn't anymore. DIS-unity.

"…(merrily, merrily) *Life is But a Dream…*" But what does that mean Death is?

Much as a Zen *koan*, these are matters that can bring the Mind back-upon-itself. That marvelous still moment when the Mind – having driven off a logical cliff – pauses to blurt out the furtive *"Huh…"*

Most people don't ask until The End, however. Because we have done what humans do best: We have made a *Business Out of Death.*

Understand my core philosophy springs from the realization that *"Everything is a Business Model,"* and you'll see it clearly. Death = Big Business.

May have started with shamans.

When a *Big Person in Village* (BPIV) died in ancient times? Someone stepped forward offering solace by means of a wonderful story to the assembled mourners. Later, people would come and thank him for the kind words.

"Hey…these dead stories sell! Bet I could gain food, power, status and do a LOT less work if I became a story-teller at times of Death!"

Thus, was marketing Death likely born. Stories of Death are much like the Tall Tales in Texas. Shamans trying to "out-dead" one another.

321,000-years too early for the rotary steam press, and no *New York Times* best-seller list to aim for? No "fact-checkers"? Storytelling worked as an oral tradition. Seen in the roots of ancient "religions."

Handing out some drugs, the stories became more powerful. The shaman's "take" went up. Shamans became full-time researchers. Smoke a little plant? Chew some peyote? The worlds in the Mind were bulldozed and re-seeded with tales that sold best.

Something else happened, too. Lots of humans had Bad Trips.

"This is what Hell is like!" offered the now drug-using shamans returning from original ayahuasca adventures. Until you O.D. on something? Warfare between hemispheres of the bicameral mind is only conceptual. Afterwards? Totally *real.*

Shaman incomes went up. More time and effort went into Product Research. More drugs. Training a *group* of *followers.* Result? The stories got better and better. Until finally, the heroes in the stories started to die. The disciples spread the story around. They did what marketers call "seeding the audience."

Of course, this couldn't be revealed because it's particularly un-*magical.* That is, until the evidence was long-buried and only rumors (promoted by none other than the *shaman class*) were all that was left. Then the immortality stories started to roll.

Remnants of the *shaman* class are with us today. Some in politics, gender studies, race theory, religions, and – oh yeah – *finance.* The fine lines between beliefs and scams begin to fade as you sit back and read the cash flow statements.

It's too simple to exist loving, working a bit, and sharing, reflecting on upright bipedal placement in the Great Scheme of Life. We need "progress." And for that, you gotta hire? Me. And you gotta vote for? Me! (Seeing how this works?) Pay taxes to? (Still need hints?)

Death is an *Industry*

Somehow, along the way, *shamans* decided to bifurcate thinking. There was more profit (and eventually *money*) in it.

"We tell the happy-ending story as if the BPIV was generally liked. We tell 'happily-ever-after stories.' But if the BPIV was a bitch or 24-deer skin asshole, we will condemn them to a horrible place full of farts, fires, and dangerous skin-eaters. Think they'll buy it?"

No shit, Sherlock. Hell of a plan.

And we're *still* buying it. Bowing down before idiots.

All but the few people who realize Death is where we go to be One and Life is where we go to all be different together. Duh. Nothing too scary in that, is there?

Still: fear is how humans teach one-another.

"Don't do THIS or your {select one} *a) clothes will catch fire, b) your genitals will drip and burn with pain, c) your airplane will stall and smash into the ground..."* Maybe not the most logically centered way to teach. We should more properly think of it as "avoidance therapy" rather than Education. Old habits "die hard" though. However slowly, though, knuckle-busting learning paradigms are losing standing in Education.

When I learned to fly, I had to recover from a spin. Not long after, that skill saved my Life. Today? Spins are out. Might scare the pilots. So too, we're raising a bravery-free crop of spiritual cattle and marching them to slaughter. Though bravery and cowardice are on sale every day for precisely the same price.

Another Warning

The scariest *realization* you will ever face is of *imminent* death.
That's because Death involves *multiple actors*. Wrapped up in
religious dogma are aspects of Jungian psychology. One
biggy is the "death of ego." Shaman classes (and parties) have
been selling that one [hard] for eons.

With a sense of adventure or dumb luck, you will have felt the
presence of Death in the waking state and made a conscious
decision "not to go there" yet. If not, your turn WILL come.
Give it time. Shamans have never produced a living,
breathing Death-Beater for Science to inspect. Like a viral
Facebook or Twitter post, it seems to track-back to fake news.

"Ye of little faith." They would argue, all the while keeping the
drugs hidden. Bar them from non-priestly class users. Go
figure. But it's all about control… A few will notice. "Fact-
checking "immortals?" Little light on the data, there, Bubba."

Consider yourself a neophyte and pretender. Facing Death
absolutely WILL scare the piss out of you. Heart will race,
won't catch your breath. Around the edges of vision, blacking
out will be noticed. As your consciousness closes in on itself,
the blackness closes down to a tiny circle in your field of
vision, if you let it and don't beat it back.

Short story. Eight or nine years back, I was doing some
welding outside my office/shop building. Too much current,
arc was run too long, and by the time I smelled the smoke
there was flame shooting out of a junction box. Threatening to
touch off a wall covered in T-111 plywood. Instant panic.

The course of action was instantly clear: Kill building power, pull a charged garden hose in and be ready for fire combat. I noticed as the action plan began the blackness around central vision beginning. Recognizing panic, I beat it back with a mental bat. Ran the plan, ended the fire, and Life resumed. $5-bucks worth of damage. $100,000 of shop building, equipment, my office with computers and electronics, suffered not a scratch.

Lesson: When you get to the edge of Panic and the vision begins to narrow even a bit, refuse to let your mind enter shutdown mode. *"Wait! What's to fear? I either put out fire or lose $100,000 worth of building and equipment…"* Then I thought *"It's all insured!"* That relieved the main pressure. Separated from the still lurking *"Worst that could happen is you die…"* No, I killed power. No source of Death.

That's when it hits you: Maybe Dying is the scary ending we've been "programmed with Avoidance Therapy" to believe in.

A useful takeaway is you don't need to fear imminent *physical* death to "Go to the Edge" as my friend Art had explained it. Learn stuff about *yourself* during your visits to the Edge.

When you've been to the Edge enough times, you'll begin to recognize it. Every time out there it is *different.*

Snippets of the visceral fear of Death may be pre-experienced (that is, tinkered with) before dying via modest drug abuse. Of the sort that follows smoking a humongous *blunt* all by yourself. The kind meant to be shared by six.
Your eyes begin to strobe. Patterns in the carpet begin to come alive. Even the very nature of Reality seems to change. Gets *drifty.* The pattern in the carpet *comes to life.* Alice in Wonderland style. Welcome to totally ripped, bubba.

Colors – once nondescript – take on a vibrance never-before noticed. *"Odd the rug never seemed to strobe and have waves in it before today. Hmm…"* Smells become *sensual* and tastes? Oh my God, how wonderful! Munchy, munchy, munch!

Eventually such experiences are likely to result in a "bad trip." In which case, your heart will pound like it wants out of your chest. Even the most miniscule noise will be thunderous. You'll be oh, so terribly alone and afraid of loneliness…*naked* before the *Entire Universe*. Ain't no *spiel* or clever lines, impromptu comedy, or flashy persona to hide behind.

To put it indelicately: "You can't bullshit Death."

After enough of those "trips to the Edge" the utter terror of it lessens. Might as well get used to it. At some time, we'll each have to go *all the way to the Edge*. And then Beyond it.

Somewhere in my 40's between the second divorce and final marriage, I got lucky. I faced Death a few times. Then? Life clicked into place. *"Oh my God! I should be packing! And I have no fear now."* So should you.

Life is a trip through the Experience Buffet Line. The more you experience, the better your "What's Next" ought to be.

So, We Move Forward

I'll try to watch my language and humor. Gallows humor is a hangover from newsroom days. Death is not fun to deal with. Language from the waterfront and the gallows humor may be unavoidable at times. Don't be put-off. We're in "direct speaking mode" now.

Since, as Bob Dylan said "…*the hour's getting late…*"

Mostly, this book is about good news and interesting possibilities. As long as you're sucking air, you can change, modify, repent, replace, relive, reexperience, rework, replant, reformulate, forgive, forget, and reconstitute that divine essence inside you.

It'll make for a better "landing" when you jump over to the other side of Death. It's a boundary, not a wall.

This book as a special "Gift." A gentle call from the Front Desk reminding you "Check-out is at Noon."

Most people will "sleep through the first call."

These are the sort who mainly slept through Life, anyway. No alarms for them. No "living on the Edge."

No challenging boundaries or "conventional wisdom."

No thinking outside the box, either. That thinking Outside the Box attitude is a sure-fire prescription for *risk appetite.* When you love risk, you're actually ALIVE.

Attempts have been made to teach risk-avoidance. Families, religions, schools. They all gang up to beat us down. And filing bogus claims on our individual rightful inheritance to seek adventure and learn risk management.

Right now? That's the Front Desk ringing. Better answer. It's
a reminder.
It's time to pack for Death.

"What do you mean *pack*?"

We all checked-in to Life with a Suitcase Between the Ears.
When we arrived, it was *empty*. As we live Life, we add things
to it. A matter of free will and choice.
Before we leave passing the boundary layer of Death, the idea
is to - get rid of as much *useless baggage* as we can. Like
clothes outworn, we all collect useless crap during our stay in
Life.

Bad habits, ill manners, gratuitous violence in movies, envy,
hate…you can work that out, right?

The Laws of Packing

These are terribly simple and immutable. This is the way Death really works at a functional level best I've been able to figure it.

1. You can't take "it" with you.

When we refer to "it" we mean *physical THINGS.*

If you had money? It's not going with you. It stays behind, so what would you like to do with your money *in absentia,* anyway?

Land? Not leaving with you, either. Who will get it? A Porsche 930? Different roads in the Afterlife most certainly. (Are *Porsche* mechanics *free* in the Afterlife? Is *that* what the "heaven stories" are about?)

Pure and simple: all *physicalities* are staying behind.

2. Death is a Head and Heart Trip

Some things are easily transportable across the Life-Death
boundary zone.

Examples? You can take your "learnings" with you.
Knowledge out of books into Mind is going with you for sure.
So are all those "personal videos" you play back in the *theater
of the Mind*. This is such a critical point we will devote an
entire chapter to it.

Feelings? Moments of absolute Joy? Load 'em in. Pain?
Well, yes, but there are tricks to packing those memories to
make them smaller and less intrusive.

3. Your Life will be Judged – by You!

Thing to be clear on? Who will be "doing the judging?"

Big shamanistic secret? YOU judge. Who better, after all?
You bring the videos, feelings, regrets, joys…you carry the
flash drive.

This isn't terribly clear in religious dogma. In fact, most religious groups do their judging in the Here and Now. I should be walking around *smoking from the fires of Hell* already! I've been sentenced by the self-righteous to "damnation in the fires of hell" for my outlook so many times. Somehow, though, I still need a jacket on cold days.

Religious groups have sophisticated "business models" which offer a product (*salvation), seek some kind of payment (*collection plates abound, remember us in your will, and the Building Fund, and….), Plus, they have make-shift product warranties citing a singular All-Powerful Being who never shows up in person for Events. Seriously? People still buy that?

You're not supposed to ask where the religious groups got their *Lifetime-in-the-Hereafter* franchise. It's like those $300 online marketing courses you can find on eBay, maybe? More marketing and sucker fishing than substance, perhaps?

They just make it up and then lie (at least partly) about it. Most took some good ideas from the heart (and competing religions) and built their business models out from there.

Not too many basic packing rules, though, right?

When Should I Be Packed?

Simple answer: *Already. Like now.* Better *yesterday*, in fact.

The first time I inadvertently spun a Cessna *Aerobat*, seeing the ground twirling 4,000 feet below me in the Kent Valley area south of Seattle (1973), the realizations came fast and furious: *"You going to follow the book and beat Death, here, Georgie?"* Hell yeah! There was no "black around the edges" fear yet. The Younger you are, the closer to Immortal you feel.

Obviously *that* one worked out. "Opposite rudder, push the nose down until airspeed is over 100 to break the stalled airfoils, then - wings level -pull back – whoa…gravity X2! *Hell yeah!*" I think all pilots should learn to wring-out aerobatic aircraft. They let you flirt with limits and piss on fear. 2G's is *nothing* in a 5G rated plane.

Another close call saw the tip of my *necktie* whip around the fan belt on top of my 911-E. The tie made just *one* flip; it was just the very corner that caught the fan belt, so it didn't wrap. I caught it before it got another chance. Whew!!!

The teaching moment there was another *monster*. Death – when it comes – is under no obligation to send an "invitation." Silly shit you don't think about kills. Invitations to Death are a matter of personal preference, though ultimately, we don't get a choice. Some are invited, some not. Death comes; or it doesn't on its own schedule. When it's *Time*.

I also stopped dismissing shop teachers tucking their ties inside their shirts in shop class as silly. Once upon a childish age, I thought that looked plain old dumb. Amazing what a 2.4-liter Porsche E can teach while idling. I still waggle arms, shoulders, and upper body looking for loose clothing when using rotating power tools. Often, there's only one "lucky shot."

Would I like to "go in my sleep" without waking up? Yes, I
believe so. Go from a Dream…what? An "expanded feature-
set Dream?" In my previous book (*Psychocartography:
Mapping the Human Dream*) I detail how we can each "map
our dream spaces."

What wasn't mentioned in Psychocartography? Fear of
immobility.

Would I like to get a terminal medical diagnosis and be
crippled for an excruciating (and unaffordable!) year on a
slow cancer burn-out morphed out? Not so much, thanks.
Dream-to-Dead would be cleaner.

Videographers have a fictitious director figure: Faye Detta
Black. (Fade to Black) mutters in production suites as a
project finally wraps. Sometimes it's a jump cut to black,
other times a very slow (minutes long) fade. Depends on
dramatic effect sought by a woefully untalented director.

Leaving life should be (ideally to my way of thinking) a result
of Honorable action, a solidly lived "Good Life" but promptly
executed with minimum fuss and expense when time comes.

That's some basic "role play" of how we go through with
Death. Which leads us directly next to the "Game" aspects of
Life…

3. What's Death?

We're all going to Die. But What EXACTLY is *that?*

Breathing stops. Shortly after the heart does. Blood flow then screeches to a halt. Brain releases some powerful drugs. These stay right in the brain because the heart is offline. One of the drugs is DMT – the so-called *spirit molecule*. Several good books are around on that.

Why pack, then? Helps to spend at least some time <u>in this Life</u> figuring out what's in your head and heart that you will take with you. Serious *hard adventuring* or a long Life will help you learn how to function under extreme - mind-shifting - circumstances. Everyone's going down that tunnel.

No conscious packing means going *stupid*. Say, you aren't going to be *one of those ignorant ones*, are you?

Joy! Life is for Living!

Ever wonder how many people have ever lived? I don't mean in New Hampshire or Kansas. I mean whole world, over all time.

According to the *Population Research Bureau:*

""Modern" Homo sapiens (that is, people who were roughly like we are now) first walked the Earth about 50,000 years ago. Since then, more than 108 billion members of our species have ever been born, according to estimates by Population Reference Bureau (PRB)."[1]

As of coffee today, 7.6 billion are alive. Therefore, we can state with mathematical certainty that 70.37 percent of all humans have already died *before now*.

In its own *odd way* this is comforting: 7 out of 10 people are already *dead*. You're just a "late liver."

If you're at a tender young age (anyone under 107) you may live long enough to see that number rise even further.

For now, however, there are *zero* cases of documented birth date humans in the United States older than 116.

A strange mathematical fact arises, too: If world population flattens out (viruses or vaccines, anyone?) the fraction of people *already dead* will increase. A big die-off and global economic collapse might push us to 8 out of 10 people already being dead. Not sure if *that's* comforting, or not.

---

[1] How Many People Have Ever Lived on Earth? (prb.org)

The number who have *beaten Death*? Sure-sure. Faith. Dogma. Beliefs, traditions. Check. What I'm asking is the number *documented in modern scientific terms*. Last time I looked? It was a Big Fat Zero.

Can we agree, this is a pretty Big Data Problem? One we might *all* want to focus on? 30 percent of all people who have ever lived are alive now, so why the data hole?

Compounding our difficulty there's little agreement on *what happens to consciousness and Mind when we die.*

Let's put that on our "shopping list." I've probably pissed-away 5,000 to 10,000 hours of study trying to answer some of the questions in this book. Here's to saving you time rounding up ideas.

How about we mosey over to the Thought Experiments Department?

The "Life-Game Simulation Model"

Recent work in physics and mathematics has proposed a wonderful "purpose" to Life.

Imagine it as a "Computer Simulation," experts in mind sciences (and math) propose.

Wrap your head carefully here: What if "Life" is a game?
And its continuation (next level up if you're a *Mario Bros.* fan)
is "Death."   If there's anything to this, Death then becomes a
"level up" – and there's some support for the idea.

Pick it up (with your mind) and let's see what this "Life as a
Video Game" looks like. Here's the User Manual to study:

4.   Life (the Game): User's Manual

A superior interactive game experience.

(Including useful hacks)

Game Warnings

- Playing as an "active player" is not recommended until you have reached 18-years of age.

- This is a simulation: modeling what's likely True about many things. Life, Death, Spirit, Meaning, and most importantly, how to successfully play the *Game of Life* itself.

It is not the intent of the Game programming staff to disparage any culture or religious order. Our high-level Game programmers are strictly egalitarian. However, in any particular *room* in this game, unfairness and injustice are critical plot elements. You just gotta roll with 'em.

Misery, poverty, heartbreak, and incomprehensible quadratic equations each seem to be special remnants from Hell (our first released game, see Life: RC1). They have been evolved in the current Game as learning tools. The help active players evolve.

History of the Game: Recognition

The Beatnik philosophers anticipated many of the rules in this User Manual. You're welcome to investigate their conclusions. However, don't blow out your liver or get lost in "the smoke." Addictions obscure the rules.

Alan Watts (*The Book: On the Taboo Against Knowing Who You Are*) and Ram Das (*Be Here Now*) deserve special mention for their high-quality gamer insights. Toss in a read of *Tertium Organum* by P.D. Ouspensky. A dandy intro to four-dimensional thinking.

In the quest for "durable rules" don't overlook the major religions. The Book of the Dead is useful, and spice generously with theosophical and psychological precepts from H.P. Blavatsky and C.G. Jung.

Player Education

There's a reason to avoid this course in Life Simulation until you are 18: there are more pressing and important things to accomplish than adopt strategies for a great Game Life:

- Learn all you can from parents and school. Realize it's all *programming* which can be modified later. It's still a starting point.
- Learn to play a musical instrument, do math, cook, and farm a bit. The more skills you embody, the richer this round of Life will be.
- Follow in your parents philosophical footsteps – including religion – until you discover and are fully *committed to a path more certain and harmonious with your core.*

Usually, by the time you're 18, you should be ready to play Life.

Consider this book a "cheat" – a source of ideas to move around – *on this level* (before leveling-up to Death) – in order to collect more psychical wealth.

Avoid overconcentration on Material Goods. One of the "tricks in plain sight" to playing Life is that all player gains must be carried between the ears.

As a result, when playing, you will need to make wise choices as to what matters most. Physically, a Tesla going 0-60 in just over 3 seconds is a rush. Emotionally, looking into your lover's appreciative eyes has higher point value.

Life – the Game – involves two kinds of play: Interpersonal (that is, with other players) and physical (solo activities, things, accomplishments).

5. Detailed Game Description

Number of Players: between 2 and 12.7 billion characters.

Play Environment: Planet Large Enough for all players. With game-ending limits becoming visible during play.

Expansion Space: Planet increments to 17 quadrillion players are available. However, these are not available unless some number of players advance from Level 1 (single planet) to Level 2 (multiple planet) before Planet #1 reaches the 12.7 billion player growth cap leading to quick collapse.

[In the simulation, at 12.7 billion, there are so many people scrambling to find food, air, and water that no resources are left for off-planet adventure and investment which is how the Game Expansion modules evolve. If you're not clear on this, call *SpaceX*.]

Life (the Game) is a complex 4-axis space-time, psycho-physical, missing instruction, massively interactive, immersive simulation. Users are inserted into, and removed from, the game on a semi-random basis.

Space-time domain terminology:

- The time-base for game years and days are loosely astronomical: Years, days/nights, and a local hour (based on hour angle of the local star) and divided into progressively smaller units (such as picoseconds) as a base 10 regression from observations.

- Distance measurements include a base-10 system (meters, kilometers) and a fading American system of statute miles and gallons, itself loosely evolved from the British pounds and imperial measurements. Rarely, you will encounter non-standard metrics based on humor such as the "Smoot"[2] or mathematically based vector measurements such as "radians."

Your Game Piece (e.g., *Your Life*).

- Play begins when a player's personal energy (spirit) becomes entangled with the Game Space via capture in an early gestation biomass. (We'll skip the spiritual/energetic exchange of body fluids, mind, and emotions involved. There are just certain things that are more fun to discover in game play.
- The upper limit of a game piece Life is semi-soft, which experientially makes for better ending play. Death may occur at any point. However, to move into additional Levels after Death, players need to become at least partially aware and conscious. Those not doing so may be recycled back into a fresh game piece (body) for another round of play. This is described as "reincarnation" by writers prior to the evolution of

---

2 Smoot - Wikipedia

Game Theory and the manual for this version of The Game.

- Quality of Game Play depends on whether you engage solo (single player mode) or as a team (two, or more, players). Team play provides continuation of play via the "Offspring Option."
- Highest scores are often achieved by Mixed Teams. In these, some solo activity is pursued (such as swimming), along with a work team (e.g., software development unit), a home team (a spouse and offspring) along with a community team (civic groups and so on).

Game of Life: Simultaneous Internal and External Gamespaces

- **Internal field** play involves mental activities. Such as thinking, loving, searching, inventing and other non-tactile efforts. The nominal boundary for this level of play is within the cerebellum where visualization is involved. Semi-passive inputs are allowed via external optical or aural inputs. E.g., A Web search and how-to video from Youtube.
- **External field play** includes five immersive matrices including the taste, touch, hearing, sight, and smell, along with extra-physical sensors. These often-ignored data sources comprise ESP and precognition plus other game levels.

- Game piece shutdown of physical inputs is a difficult skill involving soft boundaries. Example: Extreme pain is hard to shut down. Extreme joy is hard to remember. Conversely, meditative insights "in the moment" are hard to maintain. And so forth.
- **Mixed field play** is possible when, as an example, a mental barrier needs to be broken in order to achieve an External Field goal. This accounts for interest and a sense of multiple level enjoyment in such physical games as football, soccer, running, rowing, boxing, and Tough Mudders.3

Normal play begins after an early Player Conditioning Experience.

Player Conditioning Detail

Players must become "aware" to Play.

Before normal play begins, all players must complete 5 to 25-years of game "conditioning." This process consists of curriculum on the temporal axis of play:

- The Conception and Birth sub-game. (Born)
- The Childhood and Familialization sub-game. (Raised)
- The Education and Basic Skills Game module. (Schooled)
- And a Transport module. (Driving)

---

3 Mud Run | Obstacle Races | Tough Mudder | Challenge Yourself

- Optionally depending on family history, a Binding Ceremony may be involved. These are designed to "bind players" into a political, religious, or sexual viewport. (Partnering)

Player Selection Overview

Players in the Game of Life are not simple "humans".

Rather, we are ALL *transient energetics* at a level most people have a difficult time appreciating. This arises mainly from an ignorance of physics.

"The First Law of Thermodynamics states that energy is always conserved. It cannot be created nor destroyed." [Remember: The YOU inside your head and heart is a *unique energy cluster*.]

It may, however, be *modified*. In the modification process, a change from game space (Life) to non-game (Death) space is permitted. [Cheat: Yes, you are immortal. BUT your *energy perspective changes* at Death. "How?" you're wondering...]

Since the "normal" waking-state Life gamespace is a **Duality** (e.g., up/down, good/bad, sexy/turn-off, white/black, hot/cold, etc.) *its compliment* in the non-Life game space (which alive people call "Death") is a state of total **Unity**. A wholeness, oneness, togetherness, collective, and being as One.

The Art of Joyful Dying

In this book, you will (hopefully!) come to see there are several key steps to playing the *Game of Life and Death* well.

Let's take them in order, right?

1. There is a physical death. Depending on when your Life Game ends, this may be while asleep, awake, and with, or without, pain.
2. There will be a Life Review. Deeper into that in the next chapter.
3. Then comes the transition to unlimited UNITY and the conquest of space-time. All the best (*and for some, worst) of their dreams will be carried over due to packing in a non-mindful way.

6.   Connecting to Life (Game) Energy

Life Energy – the energetic force, also called *Game Energy* if you think about Life as a sim, is often referred to as *chi* in ancient Asian traditions. It's your "personal vitality; not attached to the Game in progress." If you claim your "chi" (or what a Christian might call their "pipeline to God's unlimited energy and Divine Love," you will hold unlimited power in the Life Game.

Let me expand a bit to be clear: you have multiple types (flavors?) of energy available to you as a human. When pressed, you will find some are virtually *unlimited*. Is the mental energy you hold *limited*? Actually, NO! Under the "Conservation of Energy" law of physics, you are immortal in *some* way. Sure, *form* can change. But energy doesn't go away. As Einstein explains, Life as a separate reality is a "persistent illusion" indeed!

Which raises the question "What has been missing from your *socialization and Familialization* training?" How about some basic intro to – and then leading to some initial "engineering precision" – as applied to your "personal energy?"

Is it an accident that none of us were allowed to attend *that* school?

If told today that "You have unlimited energy – just like ancient Prophets and modern Qui Gong practitioners" – would you choose to believe it, or not?

As *Johnathan Livingston Seagull* author Richard Bach noted in his follow-on book "*Illusions:* Confessions of a Reluctant Messiah" "*Argue for your limitations and they will be yours.*"

The problem brother Bach didn't explain is how we are to get away from all the embedded training that does, in fact, limit our unlimited nature. It begins with parents (I was lucky!), progresses through schools, and is reinforced depending on your places of employment and how Life (the game) rolls the dice.

Exceptional players work through these obstacles. So, let's begin to consider energy – Life Energy – from the ground up based on what we can see and sense.

Number 1: there is _physical_ energy. That's driven by lipids and sugars in the bloodstream. When blood sugars get low, adrenaline kicks in. Which burns fat into sugars, and your physical energy moves either up, or down, on that.

See a "light go on" did you? Many people who are adrenaline junkies (my son and I for sure) run toward adrenaline because it makes us "feel good." Adrenaline breaks down sugars, so _of course_ adrenaline junkies like sweets and alcohol. They get to "thread the needle" in life, how much adventure, how much booze, how much adrenaline. And so on…

Number 2: we observe that physical energy is only _loosely tied_ to the second kind of energy. _Mental_ energy. Now, it takes a moment to follow here, but mental energy IS blood sugar and fat related. People (like my wife Elaine) can get a little "foggy" when they don't eat. This is often related to, but different from hypoglycemia. It's a broader nutritional spectrum. Because while people may not be giving their brains enough sugars, there's also the need for lipids to metabolize as well. Serotonin levels matter. Coffee and steak add 5-10 IQ points when I'm tested, for example. Carbs and low grades go hand-in-hand for many.

People who _over-feed_ their bodies find that it drops into a sugar overload. They can sack out anywhere. It's also why adrenaline junkies love their carbies. Comfort food allows them to chill out. Until the urge to _hunt for the next meal_ wanders by. Then it's back to 'thrill of the chase' left over from Neanderthal times.

May not help you learn to disconnect your *mental* and *physical* energy from one-another, but a useful exercise may be (with doctor approval) *IF* – short for *intermittent fasting*. Most people eat every six to eight hours. Intermittent fasting says 10-12 hours is what you need in order to burn-through all the previous food stuffs you've eaten, plus burn-off the excess supplies that are stored as body fat.

When you do this, dieting until you burn the fat most recently stored, insulin resistance drops. Your energy stabilizes and your mind becomes quicker.

So much of nutrition is based on evolutionary adaptation that it's amazing modern "doctology" doesn't begin with whole-body metabolism work first. But supplement companies don't hold as many conferences in renown upscale vacation lands. They haven't populated the FDA with "captive regulators" either. I mentioned "Everything's a Business Model," right?

Good stuff, fasting. Why it shows up in many of the world's great religions, too. Separation tool.

Number 3: that's our *spiritual* energy. The best way I can explain the difference between spiritual energy and mental energy is to imagine them as a washing machine filled with clothes. The mental energy is what powers the washing machine. The spiritual energy is the real "work getting done." Too "far out? Sure…we can refine the idea. How about:

An Electronics Analogy for Personal Energy

While this is a book on dying well, it's extremely powerful to understand some basic electronics. The analogies are "all over Life" when you look.

Tube technology first: An "amplifier" works because a large current flow between the cathode and plate is controlled by a fine *grid* between them. A little voltage change on the grid can result in a big change in current flowing through the plate.

Now solid-state: Here, the big current flow is generally from the Collector (like a plate) to the Emitter (like the cathode). The Base does the same control function as the grid!

Hopefully, this will begin to make sense when we frame the *spiritual energy* people have as very much like their "grid" or "base."   Extremely small spiritual differences deep inside render HUGE changes in both Physical and Mental energy!

Mental energy is used making and recalling memories. Brain being (rumor has it) a 3D holographic storage machine. Its theoretical form isn't terribly complicated, though. When you fire neurons long enough and often enough, the neuron pathways "form a habit" which (*presto!*) we call a memory. Not perfect, perhaps, but the idea is clear for the taking now.

What's keeping all the habits alive? Ah…that's the physical energy. If the physical side becomes undernourished in some people, there go thinking and reasoning skills.

The "cheat" is to have a vibrant "grid or base" which can "turn up the physical" even in the absence of food. Look up Wim Hof sometime. He's a Dutch extreme athlete noted for his ability to withstand freezing temperatures. But, more than that, he demonstrates that the spiritual energy (decision, commitment) when used to control the mental allows the physical to do amazing things.

Things it shouldn't really be able to do according to limited, linear pseudoscience.

The Triad of Consciousness

Much as there are three states operating "between our ears" there are also three domains' people are resident in, regardless of being alive or dead.

The physical waking-state is one. The second (very much like the control grid or base in electronics) is the realm of sleep and dreams. The "dead part" is likely to be like a dream without end. That is, until the End of Time, but even this is debated.

Unlike our pet *Zeus the Cat*, you can (from the waking-state) choose to operate in one domain alone, in two (the alive or dead model which religionists like because it's an easy sell). Or you can follow the data implicit in *MacBeth* and spend time in all three. Trying to move between realms as consciously as you can.

Together, these *"realmscapes"* form and shape your Life Energy. If you are in good physical shape, cycling your sugars and lipids, and if you exercise the brain (forcing it to constantly learn and remember new stuff, AND you work on a "long distance connection to everything else over all time" via Dream Work, then you are likely to have exceptional amounts of Life Energy.

Little changes in spiritual matters results in Big Waking and Dream state changes. Think control grid or solid-state base connections. (I want to grow up a JFET! – look it up.)

Unlimited power is there for the claiming. Might take work, though.

Since passing on heavy meals isn't going to help? Well, just this once we'll have 10 doughnuts. (My personal best was 12 maple bars. ISYN.) Moreover, since mental energy takes repetition and practice (can you say *"Boring!"*?), who wants to volunteer to do that when we can binge-watch and veg?

A "Deadly" Problem

A problem with Death is that if you are not *conscious* of your Life energy, you can float about dismembered in a sense; unbound to a specific Reality domain (e.g., extradimensional energy). If you haven't (**key stuff here**!) "<u>Claimed Your Personal Powers</u>" and consciously joined "the Life Game" you may be set up for a [spiritual] "mugging" in the AfterLife. We enter the waking life weak as babies, but we can choose to depart as ferocious warriors. Carnivores of spirit eat the weak who enter Death unawares. Fierce between the ears at ALL times and in all Realms!

If you haven't come to terms with your own, deeply held, and nourished *personal energy*, it may be claimed by disincarnate Energy Beings. Unattached Life energy arises when players turns are ended, yet they refuse to leave The physical Game Space and level-up into Death. Called by shamans the *demons* and *devils*.

Although not a frequent event, since the Life Review helps clear up so much, this unattached energy is likely responsible in Life game space for ghosts, apparitions, jinn, and disembodied spirits. Your heart (chakra - spirit energy) is your link to the Game of Life, dead or alive, and into Dreams. The Game Master's address is the crown chakra.

Think of it like you get to pack three nesting suitcases. The Big One is for Life. Middle-sized one is for Dreams. Smallest is the Spirit case. While obviously *the* most important from an *all-time* standpoint, the big one is the most (presently) memorable.

How to Best Pack?

99.9 percent of people, I'd venture, aren't even aware they're packing every day of Life. *"Oh, that thing barreling down on me? Death, you call it? Naw…not that Kenworth about to run me over. Shoot no, don't worry about it…"*

Care to guess who's setting themself up for a terrible surprise?

If you're not playing as the Game-Masters *(god(s) or *Eternity*) wishes from its Understudy (you), then a mugging and another dose of reincarnation may be applied. Attempting to teach you the lessons you've missed in earlier Life play will eventually work out. But how many do-overs (reincarnations) does it take to figure it out? Depends on the player and their level of "stuckness."

Energy Beings (like us) may, of course, be "captured" on any of the 10-dimensional levels of play.

For Players of Life in four-dimensional space, apparitions and energies may be invoked (summoned) using rituals.
However, the motives of non-game free-space energetics must always be suspect. Most are disincarnated beings who didn't move along to higher levels of play. And then you have the demons, of course.

Summoning and conjuring is inherently dangerous stuff. It can cost your entire energetic life force. Possessions are real. Your Life force can be held by dismembered spirits that have claimed more power than You. Should you not be rigidly attached to your spiritual core…oh-oh! Expect a spirit mugging.
Fierce and warrior-like is the only stance.

Once you see *that,* fierce and warrior-like in Waking shared consciousness sure looks like "unlimited energy." Because it is. You *channel* the raw power of the Universe in a very dilute fashion.

How Sex and Birth Figure In

Newly permitted Players (dispatched to the Life game with refreshened life energy/chi from being "between game rounds for a while") are born as a result of Capture. That is, the not-yet alive spirit of a New Player becomes ensnared in the bio-field surrounding an orgasmic sexual experience. This "casts a net" which under the right conditions leads to biological birth. (Orgasmic energy attracts permitted, not yet actualized Players, as should be apparent. The orgasmic coupling in the vicinity of a ready egg locks in the new spirit for Game entry. About a 9-month ride to enter.)

Additional player insights are available in the study of sex, yoga, chi, and orgone energy for advanced players.

Following the *ensnaring process* and birthing, a set of environmental values and beliefs anchor Players to the bio-web team that has captured them (e.g., Family.). The bio-web, by the way, is another example of the concept of "duality" for which Waking Life is renown and is the main orienting feature of the Game space.

Duality is HERE and NOW. Unity and the Great Flow is on the other side. Everything in The Waking Game is duality, mom and dad, day and night, rich and poor, and so on.

7.   Game Visualization Exercise:

To understand Game space, try letting go of your physicality for a few minutes. Imagine you are *solely* an Energy Being. You have unrestricted (and unassailable) *unlimited* power. Since that physical Law (Conservation of Energy) ensures your 'core energy' may never be destroyed. Change games? Change planes or levels? Of course. But a player at all times. Your energy is *immortal*. Which means *you are too.*

It's likely that you will, over many incarnations, sample multiple game spaces. Moving, as a dandelion seed (fluffy and blown on the wind) being caught in a spider's web worth of biofield in each new game domain. The present web you're in represents the Earth-level bio-organism's force field.

We have some ideas what "other game spaces" may be like. The literature (mystic, shamanic, and religious) contain descriptions. A 'heaven' outcome is highly sought-after but sounds dreadfully *boring*. The 'hellish' outcome moves into perpetual frustration, pain, suffering, and anger. But other disciplines offer alternative game space interpretations. Even some sense of continuation.

For example, there is a game space – reported via electronic voice phenomena (EVP) researchers that offers a game space where *colors* are the central aspect. Mind-boggling intensities that trigger emotions; mainly of joy of the sort bringing tears to your eyes. Color driving emotion to the heart of spirit. No "blues" please!

Feelings and the colors represented are vastly deeper. Eye-watering greens, heart-wrenching blues, and so on.

During game Play, you may notice fellow Energy Beings making false attempts to "escape" (Exit the Game) entirely. Transcending the Game is nearly impossible. Perhaps one player in a billion. Most Players are forced to either select another bio-web (after Life) for additional play or learning (refer to previous documentation on "reincarnation") to become active Co-Creators as a more useful and appropriate level of Play.

This Co-Creator level allows advanced Players to begin crafting their *own* World skins to apply to future Games such as the four-dimension world sims with names like *Shambala,* and *Nirvana,* oh, and Dream. Where they will have carried ahead the best imagery of the present game space as an ideation for future game play foundations for development. Players readying for this level are likely to spend some of their "sleep" periods in vivid and lucid dreams in training.

Game play may be halted any time. (Death, player evaluation, and future play decisions then follow. The normal path is [replay or next level up].

The Present (Planet Earth) Game space has been in general Play for more than 5.6 trillion years. It is played – as a massively networked game - all across the Universe with assorted Game Pieces and settings, depending on which planet the game is played on.

Game Entry and Loops

Players must consciously enter the Game in order to play.

This may be done at random as a player Ages. Some will not enter the game at all and will exist on the External Field or as non-connected pieces. Be aware, however, they may be involved in a different Game Session. Use discretion when interacting with other players when discussing the larger Game of Life path.

Most aware Players will engage *both* the Internal Field and External fields of play. By convention, there is a usually 8-hour period of non-play provided daily devoted to free-running of the Internal Field (dream states) for resetting of conceptualizations and to recharge the Energy Being. This period is referred to as sleep.

If you seek additional clues, need to communicate with the SysAdmin, or seek additional documentation, select "Meditation/Integration" from behind the eye lids menu structure which you will become aware of over time.

This menu is activated carefully *between waking and dreaming/sleep.* A second menu opportunity exists upon return (moving to waking *from* dreaming) but it's harder from here. Practice waking slowly – over several minutes. This allows time to bring learning from dreams into the waking-state world. Similarly, going the other way (*into dreams*) is best done slowly as well.

Ask "What lessons do I take from today into Dreams on this visit?" when going to sleep. And, which on rising, becomes the question "What can I bring from the Dream Realms into the waking state that will be of use?" You'll find precognition follows you into waking from dreams with an occasional prompt from the SysAdmin.

Strategies, Basic

There are two essential Methods of Play,

<u>Type One:</u>

This level of play is usually a novice player who has not been in the Game as long as others.

Type One players are mainly still mastering the External Fields and may not be prepared to take up a second position of Internal Play.

<u>**Type Two:**</u>

Players, usually with several iterations of playing experience (or reincarnations/restarts into the game) and some success at External Play, will move to Internal play for a variety of reasons.

The main one is that the Internal Field is where *Transportable Game Credits* are collected. These have been incorrectly called Karma in some texts which have attempted to describe the sim without proper language. It is the currency system in the game.

Upon Death

The game of Life ends when the following has occurred:

- The player's biological host is no longer operative.
- The Energy Player has agreed to "return to Source."
- And the Player is willing to leave the game's "good-bad, up-down" mindset (called *duality*) and return to the general case (where it's all One, Unity, and somewhat homogenous).

There is *some suggestion* for people who have explored electronic voice phenomena that there's much more *intense color* in the Unity state, as well. Tactility downplays and heart chakra energy powers more than in the Life sim.

Getting back to which… At the conclusion of Play, each Player will provide a playback of their entire Game experience. While a review committee may be present to watch, the Player is given the opportunity to self-score their own effort in the game. We'll run through this, but one more chapter of learning first.

---

8.   Tapestries, Viewports, and F-Stops

As the reality of being – even in some small measure – an *Energy Being* seeps into your understanding of present life, you will begin to change.

Just as a woman cannot become "a little bit pregnant" – the instant of accepting you are an *Energy Being* – trapped in a game space (*Life) – you can't simply be *'a little immortal.'* You are, or you are not.

If you dream, you may have visited another game space. Perhaps even many times to the *same space*. I wrote extensively on this point in my book "*Psychocartography: Mapping the Human Dream.*"

Guidance in the afterlife is no longer the exclusive domain of religions and philosophers. It may come from science; it also comes from ascendant people who "get it."   It's a data structure. One that is constantly evolving.

Here's one of my favorites, as long as we're considering dream space as a training area: *"If a man can bridge the gap between life and death, if he can live on after he's dead, then maybe he was a great man."*

Know who said that? James Dean. Teenage heart-throb actor who died in 1955 after playing the lead in *Rebel Without a Cause*. He was cast with Sal Mineo and Natalie Wood (*all long dead). Metaphorically, Dean was, I believe, telling us oodles about the Game of Life. Maybe we don't need *causes* (*religions?). Maybe the Game just *is*.

If it's anything like a *simulation*, why name the database you don't have credentials for? Your life is a series of discrete database records. Not full CHMOD administrative rights.

The Tapestry Lesson

The Game of Life is an ever-evolving tapestry. You know,
        "tap·es·try
/ˈtapəstrē/,noun: piece of thick textile fabric with pictures or designs formed by weaving colored weft threads or by embroidering on canvas, used as a wall hanging or furniture covering. As in "paneled walls hung with old tapestries."

Each of us may be envisioned as a *single thread* in this view of "the Game." The length of the thread being the length of our lives. Nearby adjoining threads will all be necessarily different than us. Each having its own length. Each fulfilling a role.
At the entirely self-absorbed level, we don't need to interact with surrounding "threads" of Life.

Yet nevertheless, as we zoom-out – seeing many more threads as our zoom-out builds – we can notice local "themes" appearing. Colors group. Themes and directions appear. Zooming out even more, an entire story can take shape.

Which is how a simple tapestry reveals we are all individuals, yet we're all telling a story of some sort. Idiots in school, is it?

A quote appropriate to the period when tapestries were all the rage amplifies this perspective. Shakespeare's *As You Like It*, Act 2 Scene 7: "*All the world's a stage, and all the men and women merely players.*" Are we each CGI-game sprites in The Game?

Oftentimes, it's hard to remember we're all just players. Threads in a bigger story.

Nothing wrong with "self-absorption" of course. Social media wouldn't exist as the largest rat hole and timewaster in history without it. However, turning off social (and all other) media reduces the ambient noise between adjoining threads. In peace and quiet, we can hear one another. Enabling us each to draw back a bit and consider the picture this tapestry portrays.

The "Thurow Viewport" Lesson

Unless you have grappled personally with digital web page layouts (arrangements of responsive code under HTML5 and such) the concept of *viewports* may be a bit foreign. Similarly, unless you have read (Dr.) Lester Thurow's economics book "The Zero-Sum Society" (1976), the idea of everything offsets *somewhere* may be unfamiliar, as well.

Let's fix that with the "viewport" concept.

At its most elementary level, "A viewport is a polygon viewing region in computer graphics." Most frequently viewports are encountered by the non-programming population as "In web browsers, the viewport is the visible portion of the entire document. The part before you scroll down to see the *rest* of a page."

If the document is larger than the viewport (whatever your monitor is set to), the user can shift the viewport around by scrolling.4"

The second core concept is the book "*The Zero-Sum Society*" by Lester Thurow. The book is useful at two levels. First, obviously, is as an economics book:

> "Interpreting macroeconomics as a zero-sum game, Thurow proposes that the American economy will not solve its most trenchant problems-inflation, slow economic growth, the environment-until the political economy can support, in theory and in practice, the idea that certain members of society will have to bear the brunt…5 '

---

4 Viewport - Wikipedia
5 https://www.basicbooks.com/titles/lester-c-thurow/the-zero-sum-society/9780465085880

Hold onto that point: Macroeconomics is a *zero-sum* game.
One where you have winners AND losers. But it <u>all</u> *averages
out to zero.*

"Hold it! What do you mean zero-sum game?"

Hmm. Start with the U.S. Economy. I had to work harder,
longer, and can't afford *as good* a retirement as my late
parents. The productivity of America's good. It's just there
are so many more people for the sociopolitical system to take
care of retirement life is already in decline. As the number of
people not-yet dead increases, the speed at which Social
Security goes bankrupt will speed up. Zero sum: Only so
much to divvy up.

"Plandemics" can slow this. With the right combination of
diseases – attacking only those age 65 or above – and focused
on the poor? Well, clearly that's a Social Security Fund-saving
disease. Accident waiting to happen, or already in play?

Let's look at this as a game development programming
problem: How do we have a massive interactive game yet *not
load down the Central CPU* with quintillions of minute
decisions? Without constantly loading "Judgment code"
everywhere? The answer? Have Good and Evil, Up and
Down – all those polar opposites *balance out* the majority of the
time.

Observe how the G.O.D. (*graphics operations department)
has tons of spare time and processor overhead now with this
change? The G.O.D. in each of us can sit back and appreciate
game flow. Implied balance means we become *exception
driven.* (Or, in computer terms, interrupt driven.)

The second level comes from extensibly thinking on how the
"zero-sum" concept works in Life (the Game).

A Few Examples

A couple of years back a murder took place. A person was killed. The cops caught the perp. A trial was held. A lethal injection followed. The murderer is dead. (We got stuck with the bills for all this activity.)

In a sense ("...*an eye for an eye*...") you can behold how a kind of zero-sum was achieved.

Future murderers may have noted the death and were put on notice that "*If they kill, THEY will be killed...*" Crime prevention at its most basic is swift and certain punishment. This simple fact is something (ultra-liberal) political whack-jobs can't seem to realize. Their delusion is the game can be unbalanced. Yet as sure as double-entry accounting, in the Duality World, balance is maintained. But I digress.

When the potential for profit from crime is consistently less than the "ultimate cost" (*punishment involving a needle) then there is little (*or no) crime.

Vexingly (as I wrote in another one of my books) crime in today's world has been *industrialized*. Weak punishments exist that actually *generate* enough crime to employ a huge fraction of the population in law enforcement and the judiciary.

With an *even-larger* portion of people willing to pay higher taxes to avoid becoming crime victims. Good people balancing off bad. With higher taxes (bad) for better security (good)…the litany runs out hundreds of decimal places.

Sweet racket, huh?

We can see, using Dr. Thurow's extensible *zero-sum* thinking that every human interaction holds zero-sum potential *when our viewport is properly set.*

Imagine next that a man and woman fall in love. They "capture another Game player" one night during sexual congress. The sex act "sets the spirit energy web" trapping another soul into our Game space (is this why sex feels so good?) . A child is born 9-months later. This boy grows up troubled, but the parents are loving and attentive.

With the viewport settings only broad enough to show a difficult child, we can't see beyond what our "bounded thinking" (viewport settings) allow us to see. However, when we remember the Lesson of the Tapestry and how to use our viewports and especially when we go searching for "zero-sum outcomes" we can hypothecate several possible eventualities.

When we zoom out to "tapestry view" we can see one future where the troubled boy finds himself and shakes off a bad "early game." He then goes on to lead a heroic and prosperous life. Or he becomes the murderer in our first example.

Each of these possibilities then triggers logical knock-on effects. Life is a chain-reaction game. The tapestry is always printing. Few play it this way, though sociopaths can prosper. Especially in sales When chaining events are doggedly pursued (*it's a complicated sequence of chain reactions) assuring we will eventually get to a zero-sum ending.

The joy to all this is the sure and certain knowledge that no matter how *bad* an event is, there will be a countervailing *good* somewhere down the reaction chain. The bummer? The opposite's also true: That no matter how much *good and joy* we introduce, the zero-sum nature of Life is that a *painful bad* will balance it off somewhere. The tapestry of Life prints happiness and fades back to averages. Or prints disaster yet recovers to its graphic central tendencies.

The trick to a happy life, then?

Instinctively twiddling with your viewport focusing on keeping "good" on your "page" of the Game. Coupled with the deep realization that monks and aesthetics choose to live apart to remain free of involvement and attachment to "reaction chains" that distract from their efforts to understand The Game itself.

One of the secrets of which is that Life is a communicable disease.

No surprise there: Elaine and I have been sitting out in the woods convinced aging and death itself is a communicable disease, too. That was implicit in the pandemic, was it not?

F-Stops and Depth-of-Field

Two more useful tools for "opticizing" playing The Game of Life well. Both are from the field of photography. From the long-ago era of tintypes and contact prints. Long before charge-coupled devices (as in CCD camera technology).

F-Stops first:

The F-stop of a camera lens defines how "open" the eye of a camera is. Except instead of "open" or "closed" Game complexity requires the term *aperture*.

"In optics, an aperture is a hole or an opening through which light travels. More specifically, the aperture and focal length of an optical system determine the cone angle of a bundle of rays that come to a focus in the image plane.6"

Let's talk for a moment about where your physical game piece (body) has f-stops. There are stops associated with each of your five senses.

- Sight's f-stop is obvious as the iris closes down in response to bright light.
- Taste's f-stop is shutting down (or opening) in response to food tastes and textures. Spice closes down the stops; sherbet between courses in a complex meal opens them up.
- Touch has an "attention f-stop." When you are reading, you unconsciously close down your "touch f-stops." You don't feel your body. Body attention frees

---

6 https://en.wikipedia.org/wiki/Aperture

up more mental horsepower to focus on other input. Hammer your thumb and the F-stop slams open in pain.

- Hearing has a f-stop similar to the automatic gain control (AGC7) that turns down apparent sound levels at rock concerts and turns up apparent sound levels while "listening hard in quiet woods." ("Hear that? Was it a Sasquatch?")
- Smell (closely related to taste) has its own f-stops, too. Something too *pungent* or irritating (the smell of certain chemicals, for example) triggers discharge of nasal protective fluids (snot) to keep your smell sensors from overloading. ("Smell that? Is that a Sasquatch?")

Pulling It All Together

Our "game pieces" *seem* relatively straight-forward. Mechanistic perhaps. People – those other threads in the tapestry – are a little more complicated. We're all linked, and the Game is non-stop continuous play, so that's all fine. No one notices the zoom-outs.

Part of this is a defense mechanism. As we get more focused on ourselves, we can "turn off some of the bad" going on out at extensible levels to make Life a zero-sum game. Turning off "bad" in your life moves the zero-sum *up*, in a sense.

---

7 https://en.wikipedia.org/wiki/Automatic_gain_control

We can also manipulate circumstances (and our own measure of enjoyable Life) by retreating from areas of bad/evil/pain/suffering/loss. Distribution of good and bad in life are uneven (and maybe even Gaussian[8]) distributions. If you consciously gravitate towards happiness and good (service to Others in the Game) you'll likely enjoy a much better "playing experience" than people drawn to bad people/evil/pain/theft/and violence.

It's just how the game works.

Last, a little secret. From reading various adepts and religions:

The channel of communication between your Energy Being and the present physical Host Body (*game piece) seems to be the Heart chakra. You can feel it at times of extreme joy as well as pain. You have maybe felt your "heart swell with pride" or suffered a "broken heart" from failed romance.

The exercise I enjoy most (this may be a "cheat") is periodically using the "pipe command" to periodically connect each of the five senses directly to heart, and thus, higher Energetic Self.

"Pipe Command?"

Sure. From its abbreviation when you want to redirect IO in programming.

---

8 https://en.wikipedia.org/wiki/Gaussian_distribution

"In Unix-like computer operating systems, a pipeline is a mechanism for inter-process communication using message passing. A pipeline is a set of processes chained together by their standard streams, so that the output text of each process (stdout) is passed directly as input (stdin) to the next one. The second process is started as the first process is still executing, and they are executed concurrently.9"

Mastery of your personal "pipeline" commands is incredibly rewarding, but also a little disconcerting.

For example, when I listen to audio in our home studio (16-tracks, 128-mixing, nothing complicated), my "immediate mode10" is that of a broadcast professional. Emotion is turned well down or even *off*.

However, when a project is complete, I "pipe" the final listen to *my heart chakra*. Where the real worth of the effort is assessed.

As a result? I can listen to *anything* as a stone-cold detached game piece. Or I can be reduced to tears by a fairly short passage in an orchestral track.

Man with great heart? Shh. Don't tell anyone. My "game taw" is that of a hardcore adventurer. While that's true, the "spiritual being behind the curtain" is a sniveling softy.

---

9 https://en.wikipedia.org/wiki/Pipeline_(Unix)
10
https://www.definitions.net/definition/immediate+mode#:~:text=immediate%20mode(Noun),display%2C%20contrastin g%20with%20retained%20mode.

We hide that aspect of self, except from ones we love. Because In the Game, other players cannot be trusted. We risk only a bit and then press ahead with snap judgments – right or wrong – mostly judging others unworthy of our deepest core.

Addictive game? Maybe. But only worth playing solo as high adventure or happily ever after with a soulmate, as I've found it.

The BIG Secret of This Whole Book

So far, it's simply this: Much as religion has sold the idea *that "God created man in his own image"* we are doing the same with computer technology. We haven't fully wrapped the implicates of this into our lives and thinking, yet.

That's because most people haven't taken the "down time" to fully integrate what we're building in the Game of Life. So, a disproportionate number of non-players or partial players (Golems) is to be expected.

But make no mistake, we are creating computers as a likeness of ourselves. And as we zoom out far enough, we can see how there's a nested design pattern for "Energy Beings" to go knocking about planes and realms. Spawning sprites much as we move into *Second Lives*.

We are presently exploring in dream states with our physicality's. And we are exploring alt. physicality's with our game code.

It's pretty cool, actually. Downright graceful, huh?

There seems to be a point to it all: And we call that "filming for the Life Review.

Because when each of us dies, we get a score. And we take detailed notes on every step of our Game Play in Life. We review our play. We may have a guided review, too.

Thing is, we don't run our game settings off on a SDH chip or USB stick, though.

There's ample storage in the suitcase between our ears…

9.   The AfterLife Film School

[**Reader Note | | |** A lot of my better thinking shows up on the UrbanSurvival and Peoplenomics web sites. Some adventures recounted will open your head up to the idea that "Successful Living *includes* Successful Dying" at the end of Life…]

In a Life-or-Death situation, here's a useful tool: being able to "tap-in" to almost unlimited energy. While, at the same time, remaining clear-headed and detached from what's going on around you. With this skill you can make clear-headed decisions with some immunity from calamitous events.

This is the mental dimension of prepping. We talk about the physical all the damn time. Water, power, food, garden, solar, plus a zillion shop tools and some of the finest classic ham radio gear out there. First-aid kit? Go-Bags? Sure, sure.

But strip it all away and the most important part of prepping is? Getting "between the ears" right. People – media-saturated to the point of distraction – forget here on the *"Waking War Front"* – that life is **<u>a big movie</u>**.

For better, or worse, YOU are the director. What you experience is wholly the result of your "scenes" and the "actors" and backdrops you've selected.

"But *filming* for the AfterLife?"

Come along. Cocktail hour. Director's cut.

Every afternoon, about 4 PM, my wife Elaine and I kick-back and have a cold (adult) beverage, or two, or….

When you're over 70 (as we are), it's important to take time to enjoy each other. We talk about the insane-sounding projects here. The time travel experiments, "light crowns", "speed crowns". and the next hare-brained idea "infinity bands" that are now in the works.

If the weather is cool (under 83F) cocktails are on the screen porch. From there, the panorama at our feet in the lounge chairs spreads out like a state park. 29-acres of our own private fields, massive pine trees, deer wandering through. Red-tail hawks screaming as they go about picking-off small game wandering onto their killing fields.

If it's hotter than 83? The afternoon "hang-out" becomes the "*180-Room*" – named for its 210-degree view. Don't ask about the math, lol. (This room is special to us; constructed entirely out of recycled windows from our double wide mobile home rehab.)

There we sat, one afternoon last week (on the screen porch), when Elaine asked an important question:

"Where does all your personal energy come from? You're the most energetic person I've ever met…"

My normal response would be the "shrug the shoulders"
thing. This time, however, I decided to try and explain it. It
picks up on the energetic connection with forces larger than
Death we have already touched on.

A Life Review When You Die

Sure. Life is a series of problems. BUT the Big one? We all
Die.

I've tried to "size it up" before in other articles. But here goes
another run at it.

There's been a lot of research into Death and Dying. The
most-remarkable revelations about dying – for me, anyway –
came when I interviewed Dr. Raymond Moody. Mid 1970s.
He was on a book tour just after publishing his classic "Life
After Life." This was real data. It was True Life stories about
what people were bringing back AFTER dying. When
Emergency Medicine saved the day. From this wellspring, the
notion of Near-Death Experiences or NDE's arrived.

When, because fire departments got into emergency first aid,
the number of people being "saved" from dying jumped, so
did "reports about the AfterLife."

That set-off a 40-year storm of research. It hit me hard. Like a
punch to the gut. Because Moody's findings revealed that
rarest of qualities a cynical big city news director seldom finds:
the "ring of Truth."

"My Life Flashed Before My Eyes!"

It's NOT just an old saying. There is data. Lots of data. Tons and oodles of data. Incontrovertible data. Eyewitnesses who had been clinically dead, came back, and were changed. Sometimes returned as *dramatically* better humans for the experience.

In a way, I was ready to learn this material. My childhood asthma had been so bad that several times I'd been taken to the hospital. More than once, there was a glimpse of an inviting blue light against a dark background. Not a tunnel. No, more like an escalator… My first several years of life involved *Benadryl* and oxygen. Coal tar ointments and horrific itching.

There were times – gasping for air in my upstairs bedroom – when the walls of my room would become very finely *pixelated and velvety.* There was a *sensuousness almost rubbery or plasticity* to the walls. Closing my eyes, I could see a blue light. Different from the ultra-violet germicidal lamps in my *Puretron* air filter. Less like welding lights and more powdery sky blue…

In thousands upon thousands of case-studies – when people have died and been subsequently resuscitated – there are repeating common elements. One in particular appearing cross-culturally resonated with me above all. It was the "Life Review" most reported experiencing after Death.

The research mapped it out (loosely) this way: as you die, a sequence begins – often accompanied by a humming noise in your ears.

Many returnees from Death have a clear memory, after being in total darkness for a bit, of a "tube of bluish-white light" – a tunnel or stairway it's sometimes called. That's what they're drawn to. Some experiencers report dead relatives or a guiding religious figure at this point.

Following this, the Life Review Experience (LRE) takes place. During which a "presence" – often a male figure – who may appear as a religious prophet or an "old Greek dude" will be present. This seems to depend on a person's religious beliefs while alive.

The life review – in seconds – "plays back" not only your whole life (from the standpoint of you experiencing it) but also from the perspective of others who were affected by your interactions. There's no "assignment of guilt or kudos" – but it stands (*as "filmed" in your mind) for the harshest judge there is – (YOU) – to assess and grade.

It changes people when they are brought back to life by modern medicine… They become unafraid of Death. They seem to understand more clearly the role of Love from that point forward. It's as though they have learned to "listen with their *hearts,* not only their ears. Their lives from then on – in about half of cases – are remarkably changed. Exemplary humans of higher order. That's in the data.

Many had no religion prior to their NDE and LRE. Many didn't have a *specific one* on return, either. But they became *highly spiritual in their personal conduct and practices.* One could almost call them Holy People.

Without a collection plate.

What Modern Religions Miss

The Ures don't do a "church thing" presently. I'd label myself "very spiritual" but not a "joiner." Elaine's in the same camp, too: We appreciate deeply there's "something bigger" but we're not prepared to label it until we've gotten a little closer. Data collection continues.

There's another reason for our lack of commitment: because so many institutions exist to continue "selling subservience." Bluntly, many seem to be running a "spiritual shakedown" operation. Few get into real "problem-solving" or "teaching deep love."

Worse is the conflict and we *both hate conflict*. When stagnant organizations set off marrying the oldest human learnings (such as religious texts) and find incompatible modern data retrieved thanks to medicine, they fall apart.

Too much "prophet positioning" – and sure, we "get it." Not our cup of tea, though. Not our film. We like the "science-based" approach. Read what explorers who have "crossed-over" and "returned" have to share.

Over the years, I've evolved through several approaches to spiritual matters – based on the data. I'll tell you where I've gotten today. Then some "conflict" to be resolved in the Game of Life framework.

Your Director's Viewpoint: Life's a Movie!

It's childishly simple – yet it took me many years to first figure out – and then "get right." Let me lead you – I hope logically – down this "alternative spiritual path."

It begins every morning in bed when you first wake up in the morning.

Three-step process:

Give thanks for another day. You have been allowed back on "Movie Set Earth." Where Your Job Today is to film another "episode of your Life." What do you want to see at the "Life Review" when you Die? What's the plot, featured scene of TODAY? After all, you do want the Life Review process to reveal a great movie, right?

Contemplate Your "Director's View": "Hmmm…here I am. A whole day to 'film.' So, what kind of episode would fit in here? I like heroic scenes in my Life Movie.

Will I facedown a learning obstacle? Joyfully solve a Relationship challenge? Or do we break for a documentary moment where you just watch for what "The Studio [God or Universe]" sends out from props." There are daily deliveries – people, props, monsters, diseases, love scenes…the whole spectrum…which is cool in itself! Talent mysteriously does "walk-ons" without waiting for a cue.

Might today's shoot capture a fresh interaction with one of the "bit players" in Your Life? Is there someone who will do a "walk-on" during this scene in Your Life who will bring a key lesson? Maybe it's a mash-up: a little of this and a tablespoon of that.

Check for Messages from "The Studio" or the Chief Director. Often, there's a hint about "upcoming episodes" from my Dream Realm adventures in my "other Life." The one I visit while sleeping. There, I learned that one of the key reasons for living the waking-state is to become an "understudy" of the Chief Director.

In other words, we are each empowered to "film" really GREAT Life Reviews. Sadly, not everyone "gets this" so they go off wasting their "film of Life" on really crappy material. No long shots where they zoom out and take in the grandeur, no close and inviting love scenes. But frankly *boring shit* of the same old "stuff of Life." Frames of memory that are hardly worth developing, see? Cecil B. DeMille would turn over.

Personal progression of the "soul" – which is *your* eternal "Director's Viewpoint" – comes from constantly working on your craft of Life Review filming. You wake up totally energized. Can't wait for the day's filming to start. As you doze off at night, you play back the really good scenes. They're your "daily rushes." Will it look good in "Your Life Review" film?

The Studio (and Chief Director) provides unlimited resources, too! Money, other actors, and always sufficiency for what you should be "filming."

In fact, even if you DON'T think you want or need any extras or events, they MIGHT be delivered by the Director in Chief anyway. Because the Game of Life involves a multi-massive simulation where every player is not *only involved* in *filming your Life Review* but is also *actively working on their own student rolls of film, too!* The Studio Chief is busy! Like running an ant farm with every ant wearing a *GoPro*.

Strange game space, huh?

Grasping the BFSOL

Since we're all in this BFSOL (Big Film School Of Life), the Big Studio will send in events, other actors, to put us in unforeseen or unusual situations. Life is a Game, but also a school; a point that cannot be overemphasized.

Everyone – each day we wake up - can choose to work *in harmony* with The Chief Director. *Or not.*

I find what works best is "working with The Studio" – going with the flow – rather than trying to "direct my way around the send-in's." The Director in Chief (chief programmer of The Game?) knows what they are doing more than we film school students.

Shooting for Very Personal Excellence

As you lay in bed, rolling around how you want to "film" the day ahead tomorrow morning, a lot of changes come over you. For me it's simply this: Unlimited Energy. Life is a "season", and every day is an "episode." My "job" is to film. We should all be incredibly *grateful* for the opportunity and the "camera in the mind" to capture its vibrant essence.

I almost spring out of bed. (You will too when you internalize the task deeply.) There's filming to do and although you are a bit "detached" now. once you appreciate Life is a Camera, there arises a kind of "channeling of power." You're filming for The Studio. Understudy to the Director in Chief, no less!

I knew some people who founded the "Gratitude" movement some years back. That's a great way to "film the day." Film like you're hosting the Studio Chief's review of your rushes when the Life Review takes place. *"Standing with a cup of coffee – looking into the deep woods at sunrise – can you just feel the massive interplay between all the sets going on worldwide while HERE there is peace among chaos?"*

Sucking up to the Director in Chief? Can't hurt, near as I can figure.

We don't need to "join" any political party, ideology, financial strata, or anything of the sort. We're all "film-makers." I'm filming for me. You are filming for you.

There is clear singular ownership of your upcoming Life Review film. Mine's an adventure documentary. The way mine "plays back" involves overcoming lots of personal challenges when young, learning multiple skills and then employing them to benefit myself and others. Staring down Death a few times along the way. Becoming accepting of others; even those unaware they are filming. Not my job to spill the beans because it's *their* experience.

Should someone ask? Oh, tapping unlimited power and sharing that, well, *no problem.*

10.   Prepping "Between the Ears"

In a psychological sense, is the most "freeing" thing you'll ever do.

Take, for example, when someone in my life does something intended to "hurt" me. The Director's View looks at this "actor" (or situation) as bringing *their* drama onto <u>MY</u> set. However, since I am the director (it's MY life review film, remember?), I claim ownership of the set. Whole set. It works like I – the local scene director say – or you get marched off the set by Security.

As a Director in Training, it's MY totally reserved right to accept or reject any drama that shows up around me uninvited.

"No, no, no…my Life Review Documentary is not about <u>your</u> drama…so you hang onto that and use it in your own Life Review filming. I don't have a place for it in mine…" I try to be gentle about it. But everyone owns their own drama only so far as they choose.

This "ownership of the project" – and filming never stops – and it really does give you a very special kind of "power." You're making a "film to survive Death" after all!

You know what's equally amazing? While it's laying right there – in plain sight – many people refuse to "pick up the camera" and "own it 24/7/365." Instead, they allow themselves to be passives in the Great Film of Life not realizing that may be a pretty boring "Life Review" film. Stupid people living as "extras" when all can be Directors.

But, who knows, maybe they need to do a "victim role." Maybe some souls are just "extras" too. Depends how we squint at the Tapestry of it All.

Claiming and Holding Unlimited Power

Your relationship (being an on-Earth Director) working with The Studio and Chief Director (Universe or God) offers two things you can claim any time you wish.

The first is unlimited power to create. Get this one right and there may be another life, another script to film…and so forth. There is never "solitary confinement" for a free spirit. Hey! Maybe on a whole new world – with new laws of physics and the whole substrate!

"Wait…reincarnation?"

Oh, boy…let's avoid the religiosity quicksand, or we will go back to the 325 A.D. Council of Nicaea and the role of Origen of Alexandria and from there get into a hugely complicated discussion of spiritual transmigration versus reincarnation.

Remember what this little subset of religious philosophy argument is called?

"Metempsychosis is a philosophical term referring to the transmigration of the soul, especially its reincarnation after death. Generally, the term is derived from the context of ancient Greek philosophy, and has been recontextualized by modern philosophers such as Arthur Schopenhauer and Kurt Gödel; otherwise, the term "transmigration" is more appropriate…"

See why we don't go there? NDE data is screaming "Look over here, you idiots!

The second claim critical to assert any time – any time you want - is absolute creative control. It's YOUR Film. Whole shitteree. Yours. It's what you take to the grave, the "Big Sleep" and who knows? Maybe even the Judgement Day Awards.

For now, though? Just capture good film.

Waking On the "Right Side" of Life

Let me recap the practice for you.

On waking, after the data migration from Dreams to Waking state (including visions of Future) you simply appreciate the enormous power of The Studio – and Chief Director. It's TOTAL. Remembering your camera never stops during the day's filming. You're to be respectful and accepting of any "walk-on's" who show up. They will reveal during your filming whether they are useful in Your Film, whether they are trying to drag you into a Drama they're shooting. Or maybe they're those mindless *extras*. A few will show up in your life who are Award Winners and really add zest to your Life and Film.

Elaine is my *Monroe*. She just doesn't remember it some of the time.

As a result, by the end of the day's filming, you'll have "another great one in the can" for Life Review. A successful season is made up of great episodes. Just like on TV but transportable and durable past Death. Try that with a *GoPro*. Before you get the USB plug-in update.

Which leaves the final steps (as you're heading for the potty and coffee soon after…). You begin "roughing out your shooting script for the day" – which then becomes a smooth workflow and transition into Day Planning.

Process: {In Your Director's Eye View}

Where did the plot of my Life Review Film leave off yesterday? [Remember]
Today is a blank roll of film.

What kind of episode to I want? [Describe]

What are today's main scenes you want to nail? [Jot down]

What's the shooting schedule? [Time blocks]

What props (tools, preparation) will each require? [To-do list before shooting]

Which actors need coaching? [Emails and details plus phone calls]

Where might The Studio or Chief Director send in "surprise walk-ons? Surprise situations to catch you off-balance? Strange Acts of Studio?"

This last is fun: used to be called Acts of God. That was before filming.   The Studio or Chief Director might send in a traffic accident or a winning lotto ticket. Just depends on Studio mood (and feedback). The Chief Director runs a balanced film festival. Everyone is filming! It's spectacular to grasp!

Imagine a PCR big enough to capture in detail 7.6 billion immersive game sessions! Wow.

I hope you can see how incredibly easy Life is (and plugging into unlimited power helps!) with a *Director's Eye*. And especially with unlimited "Studio Backing."

Jumping out of bed and running 110% all day is the easiest thing in the world. You know my life is an action-adventure. But I like mixing it up: some non-fiction documentary, several sides of romance. Even an ecology film since we live on a tree farm with solar panels.

The overarching Big Idea is getting in charge (and owning) your Life [Review] Film captured with your "mind's eye lens." It totally energizes every waking second.

Remaining consciously plugged-in to the unlimited backing of The Studio and Chief Director is the key action step to "Packing the Suitcase Between Your Ears."

Now, you have a choice: Do a "walk-on" today? Or is there something else to be filming right now? (It's OK to be an "extra" in my "film." See if the Great Director sends in props or set changes, too!)

All depends what you want on YOUR Life Review roll.

Just don't forget: Critically watch the "rushes" tonight as you roll off to sleep…All the rushes from every day of your life (and this is amazing!) fit in the suitcase between your ears.

Advanced Study

If you would like to wrap your head into Life as a Film School a bit more timidly and without such a high level of ownership, check out the Robin Williams movie: *The Final Cut.*

Wikipedia lays out the plot this way:

"A brief introduction describes "cutters", who edit the collected memories of the recently dead into feature-length memorials that are viewed by loved ones at funerals. Their code forbids them to mix footage from implants, to have the requisite implant, or to sell memories.

The film opens with Alan Hakman as a child (Casey Dubois). While visiting a city with his parents, he meets another boy, Louis (Liam Ranger), and the two bond as they play together. Louis reluctantly joins Hakman in exploring an abandoned factory, and Hakman crosses a wooden plank suspended high above the ground. Goaded by Hakman, Louis also attempts to cross the plank, but he loses his confidence and falls. Hakman races to the ground and panics when he steps in what he thinks is Louis' blood. Hakman flees the scene and tells no one what happened. Later that day, he leaves the city with his parents.

Years later, the adult Hakman (Robin Williams) has become a skilled cutter who specializes in editing the memories of controversial people into hagiographies. When Fletcher (Jim Caviezel), a former cutter, confronts him at a funeral, Hakman describes himself as a sin-eater, who brings redemption to the immoral. Fletcher offers him $500,000 for the memories of his latest client, wealthy businessman Charles Bannister (Michael St. John Smith), but Hakman refuses. In a later meeting, Fletcher demands the memory recordings so that he can use Bannister, who he suspects was a pedophile, as a scandal to shut down EYE Tech, the implant manufacturer. Hakman again refuses, and, worried for his safety, uses his knowledge from memory tapes to shake down a shady criminal for a pistol.

As Hakman works through Bannister's memories, he encounters a scene that implies that Bannister was molesting his daughter, Isabel (Genevieve Buechner). Hakman wordlessly deletes it and presses on. He eventually comes upon a person that he is convinced must be his childhood friend Louis. Excited, he sets up a meeting with Bannister's family to find out more information. Bannister's wife Jennifer (Stephanie Romanov) is dismissive, but Isabel reveals that the man, recently dead of a car crash, was a teacher named Louis Hunt. Hoping that Hunt had an implant, Hakman organizes a break-in at EYE Tech, but they have no record of Hunt. Instead, Hakman finds a file on himself, which he is surprised to find documents his parents' purchase of an implant for him.[11]

I'll be careful – so as not to spoil the plot for you giving it *all away*.

Just think of the movie as perhaps a source that helped to stimulate an old man's brain into cobbling up this *Life is a Film School* and the shooting for the *Life Review Experience* is our personal Grand Opening into the AfterLife.

It's the news reel you walk into the theater with. It's played just before *whatever is played Next* in the Afterlife.

We know the Order and we know (at least from our perspective) that the "feature"
film following this will be a lot longer. I mean potentially? 90 or 100 *years* versus *millennia…*

---

[11] https://en.wikipedia.org/wiki/The_Final_Cut_(2004_film)#Plot

11. An Introduction to Destructuring

Before dying – absent a real-life Near-Death Experience – many people wish to "sample" what Death *might* be like. In order to do so, substance abuse (drugs, alcohol) and meditative practices all get their fair share of dilettantes who are curious to learn "What's in their mind" that will form, shape, or drive their AfterLife experience.

By now, you have probably figured out that I am a "very strong man of Faith." Not as a result of any particular church or religious beliefs. Rather, it's the result of steadfastly *looking at available data* and following where it leads. With the data held in hand, and a "gateway changer" in the other (Filming Life), plus mental toughness to call-out "BS" on yourself, slow progress might be made towards appreciating what MAY be ahead.

No less authority than rigorous *physics* agrees that energy can neither be created, nor transformed. Which laughably ends any conflict with *religions* except insofar as they are both forms of Duality employing *monetizations* based on up/down, good/bad, and God as Particle versus God as Wave. Trivial negotiating points. But, when the future of 7.6 billion souls hangs in the balance, partisanship doesn't leave peacefully.

It's also why the Colt single-action Army revolver first produced in 1835 was laughably named the "Peacemaker". You catch the glint in other people's eyes, now and then. Prospects of fortune seem to light 'em up, Bitcoins, real estate deals, free lunches, and especially Gold. Aye, there're fevers that sweep through populations of people stuck in Duality. Fewer quest after Divinity and a thirst to know Universe. Such is the power of the Game of Life's illusion.

Instinctively, we all sense that in *duality*, for "*me to have*" implies someone *else will* "*have-not.*" Since the Truth of our Film Director (and non-stop *GoPro*) between the ears is hard to remember under a barrage of consumer messages, wars become justifiable. We "impulse build" like crazy with little inspection and no building department checking plans and permits. We wander lost until found by a collection plate group.

Blah, blah, blah.

Drawing back a way, we begin to see all of Humanity is presently engaged in a headlong rush to violate one of the oldest prohibitions on personal behavior. We make *idols* of nearly everything nowadays. Including – thanks to *social media* – outsized replicas of ourselves.

A World of Idolatry

Missed Sunday School, did you? *Wikipedia* offers the short course on the #1 Commandment in their entry on *Idolatry*:

"Ideas on idolatry in Christianity are based on the first of Ten Commandments.

You shall have no other gods before me.

This is expressed in the Bible in Exodus 20:3, Matthew 4:10, Luke 4:8 and elsewhere, e.g.:

Ye shall make you no idols nor graven image, neither rear you up a standing image, neither shall ye set up any image of stone in your land, to bow down unto it: for I am the Lord your God. Ye shall keep my sabbaths and reverence my sanctuary.
   — Leviticus 26:1–2, King James Bible[58]

The Christian view of idolatry may generally be divided into two general categories: the Catholic and Eastern Orthodox view which accepts the use of religious images, and the views of many Protestant churches that considerably restrict their use. However, many Protestants have used the image of the cross as a symbol.

Catholicism

The veneration of Mary, Jesus Christ, and the Black Madonna are common practices in the Catholic Church.

The Roman Catholic and particularly the Orthodox Churches have traditionally defended the use of icons. The debate on what images signify and whether reverence with the help of icons in church is equivalent to idolatry has lasted for many centuries, particularly from the 7th century until the Reformation in the 16th century.

On the Protestant side, veneration and (personal) idolatry are greater taboos.

> "Protestants did not abandon all icons and symbols of Christianity. They typically avoid the use of images, except the cross, in any context suggestive of veneration. The cross remained their central icon."

Wikipedia then informs us on other views on idolatry. Such as the Muslim view:

> "In Islamic sources, the concept of *shirk* (sh-r-k) can refer to "idolatry", though it is most widely used to denote "association of partners with God". The concept of *Kufr* (k-f-r) can also include idolatry (among other forms of disbelief). The one who practices shirk is called *mushrik* (plural *mushrikun*) in the Islamic scriptures. The Quran forbids idolatry. Over 500 mentions of *kufr* and *shirk* are found in the Quran, and both concepts are strongly forbidden."

And from here, it's on to the religions of India:

> "The ancient religions of India apparently had no use of cult images. While the Vedic literature of Hinduism is extensive in the form of Samhitas, Brahmanas, Aranyakas and Upanishads, and have been dated to have been composed over a period of centuries (1500 BC to 200 BC), there is no mention of temples or worship of cult images in them."

The Wiki article on Idolatry is longer, but interesting. If you have the time, a study of parallels between *idolatry* and *advertising* would make a nice book-length doctoral piece. So too, would a Doctor of Divinity dissertation underscoring how making idols is being embodied in modern code libraries and run-times in video games!

How Does Destructuring Fit?

About here, you should be asking *"What exactly IS this Destructuring stuff you're harping on? Why does it matter?"*

Let's visit the computer programming language *Java* and find out. Dmitri Pavlutin offers a wonderful online explanation:

> "The *object destructuring* is a useful JavaScript feature to extract properties from objects and bind them to variables.
>
> What's better, object destructuring can extract multiple properties in one statement, can access properties from nested objects, and can set a default value if the property doesn't exist."

We're almost to the point – so hang in there. Just one more comment to go…

> "The basic syntax of object destructuring is pretty simple:

const { identifier } = expression.

Where identifier is the name of the property to access,
and expression should evaluate to an object. After the
destructuring, the variable identifier contains the
property value."

OK…if you must…

"Huh???"

Let's rewrite the Java idea into [plain] English [language]
syntax related with the following example.

{ (identifier) "Commandment Ban 1" } = re-expression

So, in our study of *Idolatry* we can use the "destructuring"
technique in order to expand our range of thought by
assigning additional *properties*. It's not just a simple
"command" – the object implies many properties.

Bans on Idolatry might, therefore:

- Delimit (or bound) allowable "hero worship"
- Delimit "substitute icons"
- Delimit "alternative personas as icons"
- …and so forth…

In this, we begin to sense a path for today's moderns from "Idolatry" in the conventional sense (which is generally banned) to allowable groups (Ninjas, sports heroes, advertisements, etc.) which are alternate expressions of the ban, but not specifically covered. Social Media is a dandy example of desperate people seeking meaning via self idolization, for example. Not banned, but I don't believe it's healthy at a spirit level. Encourages too much narcissism. Like Earth needs more?

That is to say a "large part of what we label Progress" has been simply taking Idolatry and jumping tracks. From the religious *training* to *marketing training*. Conceptual neighbors and both with collection plates.

Destructuring – strictly implemented – has already become long-lost: we can see how basic prohibitions (things like coveting neighbor's wife and idolatry) all have been buried by the "Modern Noise" of competing media.

Cute, huh?

In a world of information overload, quiet reflection on moral and ethical points has become nearly impossible. A fact, one might argue, that has prevented even the U.S. Supreme Court from making rational decisions at times. Easier to avoid than think-through the really tough thoughts.

Making us all victims of the *Infodemic*.

Who's George P. Hansen?

He's the author of a dandy book "*The Trickster and the Paranormal*" which gets into the processes of psychological destructuring to enable us to (for some) confront very *real* aspects of the Paranormal and Parapsychology in (or near) the waking-state.

> "*My central thesis is that psychic phenomena and processes are associated with destructuring.*"

Right off the bat he then wonders about gypsies who are gifted in knowing Future, often having a sense of things to come yet are called "frauds." While on the other side – after noticing that a lot of saints claim these same precognitive skills, he wonders whether sainthood is a fraud then, too?

> "Mediums of dubious reputation have been reported to levitate, but so have religious mystics. What's the connection?"

Most people never slow down far enough to consider such outlandish rethinking of "Modern Life." Still, with more than half of U.S. adults reporting some kind of parapsychological or paranormal event, and some on the "*outskirts of Death*" seems a lot of the "hubbub and busy work" of Life is manufactured as a means of distracting us from a wider inquiry into such basic problems.

This is also the experience Dr. Steven Greer has been running into with the *Disclosure* project, by the way. When small groups of people follow some ET Contact protocols (evolved in France) and make some kind of "contact" is it possible that ETs are other-worldly expressions of Spiritual Beings dropping by our "here and now" for some contact and to chat us up a bit?

Usefully, Hansen cites the work of anthropologist Michael Winkleman whose research revealed that as societies became more *complex* in their structures, those who would explore and engage with the supernatural side of life is diminished. New depth to the term "busy work."

New words pop up in the paranormal lexicon as we dive deeper into what Death may hold. One of my favorites is *liminality*.

> "Liminality is a term used to describe the psychological process of transitioning across boundaries and borders. The term "limen" comes from the Latin for threshold; it is literally the threshold separating one space from another. It is the place in the wall where people move from one room to another."

Which circles us back to the familiar concept of my other books; the "barrier between Realms." Most of us cross into Dreams (remembered, or not) and some fewer venture into Out of Body Experiences and its closely related remote viewing.

Are these tools used by some *Trickster* who operates hidden psychic levers of people? Or is it something we can learn of through destructuring to distill some essence or useful meaning?

Another keyword from parapsychology illuminating Death a wee bit?

> "<u>Reflexivity</u> generally refers to the examination of one's own beliefs, judgments and practices during the research process and how these may have influenced the research."

That is, does Death evolve to meet our expectations of it? If you think there's a Hell out there, does the Universe respond in a cooperative manner, equipping your "film set" with a proper hot spot by making it so? The physics problems are immense and never-ending, it seems. Are people steeped in a religious tradition welcomed to an afterlife by what they have been *taught to believe* will occur?

The answer seems to be yes – and no. The data on this point seems mixed. Extremely religious people's NDEs may be *similar* to their training and upbringing. But even people who've never thought much about (or received training) still experience a similar death process.

Philosophical anthropologists argue that supranormal events have a hard time *"existing within structure"* because the word "structure" implies *order* and *hierarchy.* Thus, psychological explorations must move a person into a headspace where order falls, where all becomes One. Much as it may in a tribal ritual.

Ure Argues this Point

I have to disagree with the philosophical types who cling tightly to the anti-structure notion. To me it doesn't pass the "smell test." It has the same ring as that 1835 patent official who bemoaned the United States would soon run out of things to invent. Lazy dualism.

Between CERN and God knows how much else (black projects/A-51, now Wendover) in the quest for quantum physics breakthroughs, we are learning on the computational side that Life's *structures* are far grander than anything we presently comprehend. The fact is structures may be <u>extraordinarily complex</u>. When left to evolve on its own, as in A.I., no telling where the limits might be extended.

We can skip the question *"Were humans and the Game of Life created merely to birth the A.I. that would eventually take over the Universe? As like an "offspring" or something?* Too big a question. Makes my head hurt.

But the Act of increasing complexity does not mean – as some lazy Marxists in anthropology believe - that structure should spontaneously disappear into anti-structure. Because that lays claims in anthropology to a God-like power to see all structure. Which, obviously, it can't. Like Critical Race Theory, this one has "clay feet" written all over it, too.

Just because one set of (highly papered) anthropologists can't recognize super-complex mathematical structures behind Life does not damn all underlying data to a mythical (duality-spawned, collision unavoidable) Reality. Looks ever-so-much like another "collection plate operation" to us. Anthropology has the answer: put our new building over there…

This all ties back to the matter of anticipated outcomes, understand. The "lazy class" of liberals can't shake the ritualistic (duality) structures of shamanism, so they insist it must be confronted by anti-structure. A space away from rigorous review and science. But that's OK with them since as nihilists, they're likely to be atheists and nothing exists after Death anyway, so how could it possibly matter?

The more aggressive (and honest) mental stance is to seek deeper underlying patterns of *The Trickster*. Then, using these, back-engineer to find structure, regardless of how richly complex or simple.

It is by this route that religion and science can reconcile their differences that humans in this world might congeal into a more homogenous mass of heart-driven brain beings. Two-bit academic revolutionaries, leading soft-headed idiots from "me-me" social spaces, epitomizes Carl Sagan's *Demon Haunted World*. The *pseudoscience* types are bent on a quest to become higher-ordered jailers of humanity.

Thus, one of the grandest surprises we all shall have answers to upon our death is that *Ultimate Ah-Ha! Moment*:

> "So, this is how it all works! How cool and graceful –
> beyond comprehension in the waking Duality state..."

Fourth-dimensional thinking (as in Ouspensky) and three-headed coin tricks.

The major note of confusion, seems to me, is that many paranormal scientists don't understand their own place in the dualistic world. Dualism hides a third of the larger Reality. Thus, they're anxious to invest and promote ideas like liminality and anti-structure; unable to see it's just another round of the up and down case. Duality is indeed the trickster. Behold the Data (Unity) and there's your answer.

To suggest that moments of liminality and anti-structure can give rise to the paranormal ignores thousands of years of human religious experience. Where transition from duality to the doorstep of the unity state is where "the magic" is. Guess lots of schools need monetizations, though. Anthro-sites among them? Which we totally get. It just happens to be wrong, that's all. Divisive gibberish.

But the world's awash in that, isn't it?

12.   Suitcase Between the Ears

I think we've established a number of useful corral corner stakes in the material presented, so far. For example, we have tossed around the notion that an evolutionary form of early *shamanism* may have been a basis for the founding of some modern "religions." Incorporating "best practices" available from tribal observation and community learnings and traditions.

Another concept, terribly important, is that Life may be a bio-computer simulation of a higher-order intelligence that chooses to operate in what we experience as "Life" but which – to a higher-ordered being – may simply amount to "noise among the bacteria in an Agar dish." We're already working toward the "digital Edge." Or, Creation, as we know it, may be a passing thought.

Yet another possibility is that intelligence is "worm-like" throughout the Universe. Could it be that as an "intelligent species" we are part of a *universal tunneling instinct* that sends Consciousness through all possible Realms of space-time; media emissaries from primitive planets spawning ameba's on up? Mastering, in sequence, the land, the oceans, the skies, and space-time itself? Which begs the question *"Is there are Starting Point?"* along with the companion *"Is there a Finish Line?"*

Just outside your "suitcase between the ears" we have 7.6-billion humans; many of which have no clue what's going on! Do we master our minds such that a computational interface – an opening or *portal* into first mental and then emotional-spiritual Realms - can be launched, ported, or enlightened into?

Conceptually, it's not a pretty slurry. Because – like it or not – that's what the Data infers.

In analytic-speak, this is a softly formed pile whose "slump cone" (to use the concrete worker phrase) won't "slump very high." Still a bit runny and more Portland Cement may be needed in waking-states.

When we die, though? Likely it will make sense. At least as much *sense* as any of the most recent score of U.S. Presidents.

For now, as long as each of us keeps that "mental *GoPro* rolling" all the time, we are free to claim - during whatever remains of life - our *directorial powers* in order to have that "perfect movie in the can" for the upcoming Life Review Experience (LRE). So seems the case data sciences now suggest.

Perhaps the longest answer to a wife's question to her husband *"Where do you get all your ENERGY from???"*

Yeah. Director on a Mission is me. Looking to do and contribute everywhere I can and the clock's ticking. I jump out of bed every waking morning amped and excited – overflowing with INTENT – determined to capture all the best "footage" of an exciting, adventurous, sharing, and rewarding life as has ever been done.

And leave some breadcrumbs behind along the way. Maybe a short-cut for future humans? We'll find out.

This is what "Packing the Suitcase between our Ears" is all about. It's where we launch from every morning as rested eyes open wide on a fresh new day. The *GoPro* between the ears has been recharged. It's ready to capture another 19-hours and who knows how many *bytes* of onboard memory.

With such exciting prospects? Such a large directorial debut ahead? Do we allow ourselves even a single, sloppy, botched recall of previous episodes?

How do we *expertly pack* for the coming adventure?

A Small Secret that's Overlooked: Our "suitcase between our ears is of *infinitely large size.*" Record and play back all you can. A lot of people get lazy in this regard, though. *"Aw, too much work!"* is the complaint.

Are you serious about building a Huge Reputation as a Producer/Director and working towards a Bigger Project in the AfterLife and the one after this? If you don't care what's next? Have another reincarnation. Eventually, you'll take to rolling film throughout Life.

Understand your shots. Write today's episode. Review past Seasons (your youth, your education, your travels, your parenting, your spousing, your present goals… See how it all fits? Tapestries and interleaving plots with walk-ons galore all simultaneously playing…we…*all over the place!* There are potentially 7-billion episodes a day being filmed. Yet how many "own their own Director's Chair?"

In fact, I've seen only a handful of genuine Life Directors in more than 70-years.

Hell of a movie set, ain't it? There's a Director's chair. Just over there. It's got Your Name on it. Yours for the taking.

How could you NOT? Honestly, though, who actually claims theirs? Then, there's who's a strong director and who are the weak ones?

Papers, Please?

As you have (hopefully!) realized, the *Life Review Experience* is now medically acceptable thinking in today's world. Startling is how the implications are mostly 'just sitting there.'

Of course, realization of the data could be labeled "subversive of the Modern Order." Since follow-on research to Moody, *et. al*, has continued to evolve, the waking-state clarity into what's going on grows. With it, the risk (and threat?) of subversion grows. Real equality. Not the contrast game: him-her, Black-White, Good-Bad, Rich-Poor games dominating the Waking Realm.

No, there's an _utter independence_ arriving from realizing and internalizing that we've been "directors before" and we've allowed this season to suck. Our seasons suck because we have allowed them to. Not as a guilt-trip to be played. Just a point of internal honesty. Because (statistically) you will see a Life Review.

Let's consider our voyage to this Big Event in the paper "**The Life Review Experience**: Qualitative and Quantitative Characteristics." The abstract:

> "**Background:** The life-review experience (LRE) is a most intriguing mental phenomenon that fascinated humans from time immemorial. In LRE one sees vividly a succession of one's own life-events. While reports of LRE are abundant in the medical, psychological, and popular literature, not much is known about LRE's cognitive and psychological basis. Moreover, while LRE is known as part of the phenomenology of near-death experience, its manifestation in the general population and in other circumstances is still to be investigated."

Many thinking-points emerge to juggle in the waking mind. Not everyone who experiences death and a subsequent NDE remembers going through the Life Review process. This is the "life flashed before my eyes" sort of thing. We don't know (in persuasive data terms) whether the experience is less than universal because **a)** some people weren't going to die yet, _anyway_ so, as a consequence, they may have still been "rolling" with their mind's-eye camera gear. Or **b)** some people _simply don't experience them._ Another choice is **c)** There's memory loss between death and dreams on the one hand and the waking-state world on the other.

The most useful take-away (as a practice) in my book *Psychocartography* was to focus on the "transition zones" between "waking" and "Elsewhere." The practice has to do with remembering your waking state when in a dream. And remembering (full-bodied and beautifully captured) the Dream Realms you've enjoyed.

Two points here: The first being the "housekeeping" in waking-state. If you watch gratuitous violence or meaningless drama (from which you can't draw a useful tool or message), then why waste perfectly good waking-state time on fictional fluff? Sorry to break it to you hard like this, but Life is incredibly special. How much are you wasting? In your Review Experience, how will you explain "I pissed most of my Life away?"

If Life doesn't seem exciting, use your Mind for a little exploring. Reaching out. Everyone can see into the future some distance. I'll try to remember to drop some technique ideas as we move along.

For now? Some people don't experience the LRE. Which moves us into the next problem: What determines Who does – and Who doesn't – have a replay?

The Abstract of the *LRE* paper moves on:

> "In a first step we studied the phenomenology of LRE by means of in-depth qualitative interview of 7 people who underwent full LRE. In a second step we extracted the main characters of LRE, to develop a questionnaire and an LRE-score that best reflects LRE phenomenology. This questionnaire was then run on 264 participants of diverse ages and backgrounds, and the resulted score was further subjected to statistical analyses."

Although not stated, we assume the 264 participants had all experienced full NDEs at some level. But you know what they say about "assuming."

Which brings us down to results:

> "Qualitative analysis showed the LRE to manifest several subtypes of characteristics in terms of order, continuity, the covered period, extension to the future, valence, emotions, and perspective taking. Quantitative results in the normal population showed normal distribution of the LRE-score over participants."

It's wildly *unfounded speculation* on my part (though fortunately, I'm pretty good at this!) but isn't it possible that *if* more people were *conscious of their filming process* more would experience LREs?

The data seems to hint that "The more people remembering their Lives are filming of LREs could actually *speed up evolution of humans.* Pretty neat reason to consciously film, ain't it?

Obviously, we don't have access to the questionnaires and responses referred to in the paper, but from a spiritual knowledge-seeker's standpoint, it would be grand to investigate areas like "extensibility of present events into the future" for example. Because this could lead to important insights into how our global futuring *(future-realization) mechanism works. And has throughout history which is adorned with seers and prophetic visionaries. At a personal level, I've experienced the process work and it's quite remarkable.

Another obvious question emerges. This relates to the high petrochemical levels in the caves of Delphi, where the "seer's of Delphi" brain oxygen deprivation may have induced a DMT-like release. Which could, in turn, be an on-ramp to the "disconnected or separated Self" states. Is this the basis for (and route of) progressive dream and trance work that sequentially leads to future visions and eventually Death visions, or the other way to remote viewing?

The dandy Abstract winds up with:

> "Re-experiencing one's own life-events, so-called LRE, is a phenomenon with well-defined characteristics, and its subcomponents may be also evident in healthy people. This suggests that a representation of life-events as a continuum exists in the cognitive system, and maybe further expressed in extreme conditions of psychological and physiological stress."

Oh-Oh! SECOND Big Secret in this Book

Is simply that the "Packing for Death" process can have very salutary effects on Aging. People who have become separated, depressed, and left feeling alone by steadily declining physical health can always *keep their cameras rolling*. This is not dependent on how busy offspring might be (who rarely visit or seek the wise counsel of Elders). Nor does it depend on actions by other "active Livers." [Not to be confused with *fatty livers*, lol.]

Once you "see yourself" as both *Director* and also the "Only Audience that Matters" (except for the feedback of others into your Life's movie during playback" then a new kind of energy seeps into your Soul.

Each day becomes special. All leads up to your own Final Scenes. Do you cower at the Exit, or do you roll with the Big Finish? (I'm into huge endings…)

Are there specific beneficial processes, then? Things we can do to claim our own Director's chair in this film of Life?

Conduct <u>YOUR OWN</u> *mini–Life Review Process*. As you put "lights out" at night, take a minute a "play back the day." How was it? Anything to work on in tomorrow's episode?

As you roll through that "grand and central station" where people transit between dream and waking realms, hold on to useful notions and work on plotting tomorrow's script into something more pleasing.

In another scientific paper, "Effect of life review writing on depressive symptoms in older adults: a randomized controlled trial[12]" the results of a guided autobiographical writing process was summarized.

This experiment was based on "Forty-five participants (23 treatment, 22 wait-list control) ≥ 65 yr. old participated in the 8-wk, once-weekly autobiographical writing workshop."

---

[12] https://pubmed.ncbi.nlm.nih.gov/22742692/

Now comes the amazing part: <u>People actually feel considerably better</u> after writing down their own life-histories! Past is gone, can't hurt you now, and if there's pain with a memory, might as well dissolve it now so it doesn't haunt your *forever*. (*Which is what will happen if it's packed in your "suitcase between the ears.") Where do you think Hell comes from, anyway? It's…*us!*

"Depressive symptoms were significantly less prevalent for the treatment group than for the control group after the 8-wk life review program (repeated-measures analysis of variance p = .03)."

If you want to improve your outlook, as a senior, consider setting some time aside to write Your Life Story. Walk around looking for great scenes and get that *GoPro* between the ears going. Add the soundtrack, the taste track and the smell track, while you're at it.

These will all eventually come to film – once we all have USB ports – but let's anticipate the technology and get ahead of things.

Or, as I've been pressing in the "Life's Film School" no need to mess with a pen when you have higher fidelity playback with that biological high-end *GoPro* called your eyes capturing to unlimited visual cortex media!

13.   Hacking the AfterLife

From an UrbanSurvival.com column I wrote in 2017 came a solid flow of research topics one of which was all about…

Hacking the AfterLife.

This is bigger than the space race.

It's one of the topics that I will be talking about on *Coast to Coast* with George Noory.

More importantly, though, it might be a way to solve the "learning musical instruments" question we were kicking around Tuesday morning…

The idea is simple:

A World of Spiritual Super Beings

Admittedly the concept sounds wild but follow me through the logic of what I'm proposing here.

We know (based on eye-witness testimony) that we <u>all die</u> and many coming back from NDEs can remember a Life Review film played. Which gives rise to a most intriguing notion. Can we "loop ahead" or "loop behind" into the AfterLife and bring some of those talents and skills enjoyed by our spirits in other incarnations either forward (or back) into the present time?

I think the U.S. government should put a modest amount of money – say $250-million, or so, into serious inner-realms exploration and discovery in the area of past life regression.

Seriously: Who wouldn't love to go through a couple of 3-hour regressions and return to the waking world with a command of three or four languages, mastery of a few musical instruments, and sure – advanced math skills which can take years to learn?

We KNOW (*since the data is incontrovertible) that *child prodigies* and *savants* do happen. But, like so much of human progress, we embrace the *fashionable* in lieu of the truly *useful.*

Where the hell are savants and prodigies coming from? And why the hell do we make bombs instead of breakthroughs in areas like this? You know – *positive gain of function* from other *lives!*

Let's talk the high-level first. This is a three-legged milk stool:

First: We have a huge gulf between people of various religious beliefs. In many beliefs there is an undertone or tacit belief in reincarnation. As we have pointed out, the technology (reincarnation) is not in dispute. Where conflict arises is over its *monetization.* Since EVERYTHING is a *Business Model.*

From the (extensive) reading I have done, the "time between lives" tends to run in the range of 1-10 years with the largest hump in the data bulging between the 3 to 5-year mark. This is why many Baby Boomers can recall World War II memories. Those born from 1943 to 1951 are candidates for War period life recall, for example.

Reincarnation is not totally contrary to Christian beliefs, either. Especially if you've read deeply into the book Reincarnation in Christianity: A New Vision of the Role of Rebirth in Christian Thought (Quest Books) Paperback – March 9, 1990.

Second: A government study and clarification of the NDE (near death experience) research would be useful to everyone on Earth. Remember, almost every religion becomes tainted – and loses any claim of Truth – the minute it becomes exclusionary. In other words, when a religious group damns any other to hell, it's selling "spoiled goods."

Data shows objectively there IS something going on around the moment of death, but whether it is, as Dr. Ray Moody explained in Life After Life: The Bestselling Original Investigation That Revealed "Near-Death Experiences" is debated. Not that the data is contradictory: It contains beautiful *harmonization of experience*. Differences relate more to "followership" and "collection plate impacts."

One line of inquiry posits that a dying brain mixes up a huge batch of DMT. Great book on point: The Spirit Molecule: A Doctor's Revolutionary Research into the Biology of Near-Death and Mystical Experiences to smooth the way into the Big Sleep.

Also closely related is this free article on the government PubMed website: "DMT Models of the Near-Death Experience:[13]

---

[13] https://pubmed.ncbi.nlm.nih.gov/30174629/.gov

"Near-death experiences (NDEs) are complex subjective experiences, which have been previously associated with the psychedelic experience and more specifically with the experience induced by the potent serotonergic, N,N-Dimethyltryptamine (DMT). Potential similarities between both subjective states have been noted previously, including the subjective feeling of transcending one's body and entering an alternative realm, perceiving, and communicating with sentient 'entities' and themes related to death and dying. In this within-subjects placebo-controlled study we aimed to test the similarities between the DMT state and NDEs, by administering DMT and placebo to 13 healthy participants, who then completed a validated and widely used measure of NDEs. Results revealed significant increases in phenomenological features associated with the NDE, following DMT administration compared to placebo. Also, we found significant relationships between the NDE scores and DMT-induced ego-dissolution and mystical-type experiences, as well as a significant association between NDE scores and baseline trait 'absorption' and delusional ideation measured at baseline. Furthermore, we found a significant overlap in nearly all of the NDE phenomenological features when comparing DMT-induced NDEs with a matched group of 'actual' NDE experiencers. These results reveal a striking similarity between these states that warrants further investigation.

Which begs the question: Is DMT a "doorway opener" drug to alt. dimensions, or a simple chemical facilitator to "ease us into Death?"

Third: If there is a way to tap into past lives (past life regression therapy) then what has been done with this so far has been entertaining but not terribly conclusive.

The point is that if we look at this as a programming algorithm, it will lead to a process (which government should fund since the afterlife is a public area of interest – there is nothing higher) going something like this:

IF reincarnation is real do NEXT (More than DMT?)

If DMT does not drive Reincarnation/Past Life recall, then, do NEXT (maps regression processes)

Map Regression Processes and define the technology.

A lot of this is being done by hypnotherapists, but – to use the corporate raider mindset – there hasn't been an effective roll-up to task multiple business units with standardized reports on how the technology can be used.

My sense is, if Past Life Regression is real, then government would have a good and proper role in working out a new national technology. Like the space race but way cooler and personally achievable.

Let's imagine going into an approved regression program.

Again, in programming parlance, it might script something like this:

> "Good morning Mr. Ure. We will be doing a standard regression with you today. Is there anything in particular you would like us to focus on? And particular skills you may have once had but seem to have missed bringing into this life?"

"Well, yeah. I have always had this vision – fleeting at times – that I was a Japanese Zero fighter pilot who was shot down in a spiraling fiery crash. But before the accident, he was an excellent pilot and wore a white silk scarf and the noise…yeah, the noise of the plane going into the graveyard spiral…that's about where I lose the recall in my self-work. Down and to the left, engine on fire. So, I would like to learn more about that past life and, oh, bring a few of those skillsets into this life…conversational Japanese would be neat for ham radio use…"

"Is that what you have in mind, George?"

"Well, I was thinking conversational Japanese would be useful – high school level, not college work. And any schooling I could bring back like mathematics from his youth…plus any musical instruments…that might be useful."

"And in the case, we have time for more than one personality is there anything else you want to bring over from past lives?"

"Well, like I said, anything language-wise, heavy on math, and oh yeah, how about being a skilled musical instrument player of some kind?"

"We'll see what we can come up with. Here, take this pill. It does not produce any of the memories. it only helps us to carry back some of your past-life skills into the present by stimulating the right portions of the cerebral cortex. I see you already use Huperzine-A – it's similar to that in terms of mental acuity coming across the deeper layers…"

"More than anything, I want to bring back useful skills.
Anything that I could enjoy or monetize. Oh, plus if there was
a past life that starved, maybe that would be connected with
eating too much and some kind of skin disease/death which
might have carried over as the eczema and any breathing
issues because of the asthma…"

> "Very good, Mr. Ure. That's a tall order. I see your
> wife Elaine is with you, so she will be your personal
> control for today's session?"

"Yes, that's right…"

> "Mrs. Ure, I need you to review these few rules that the
> regressionist insists on for the safety of your husband.
> Basically, you are welcome to record the session, you
> may write a note to the regressionist, but no speaking
> aloud is permitted while your husband is in the deep
> state of recall… Do you understand?"

Which Elaine would then sign.

Then one to four hours later, I would be back on this side of
the gray line of consciousness armed with a faltering ability to
pick up conversational Japanese – which would come back to
me quickly with the inter-life barriers down (this would be
one of the objectives of the government funding) and I would
be a much better pilot, have a lot more math skills, and I
might be a fair harpsichord player – depending on what is
brought back from which personalities of past lives.

So how can you help?

Elaine and I both want to do this – so we are looking for a regression therapist who is up for the task. One reason I took to flying so readily was I had a deeply buried memory of being that Japanese fighter pilot who was shot down in WW II. Leather jacket, white silk scarf and in a Mitsubishi *Zero*. I knew there was something most *familiar* about flying. Especially our Beechcraft.

Unlike a lot of the "feel good" books on point, this Past Life Regression Education effort is a technology fishing trip. We both want to bring back skills.

To us, old as we are into our 70's a good way – but not between the ears - there is nothing like the acquisition of new skills. We're dabbling in music. Math and languages for me and Elaine's still working on her list. She scratches on her book, now and then. Considers Morse code. Should the nails be trimmed for guitar?

Since we both look considerably younger than our calendar years, we ask a profoundly serious question here:

If a government program could find a viable way to bring skills in from past lives and treat past (bad) behaviors such that people could be more expressive, loving, creative, and able to achieve, would that be something government should invest in?

My sense is HELL YES. Sadly, they don't. Do-overs for druggies is an easier sell in the home District.

Absent political leadership (which died with President Kennedy) we're willing to spend a little money out of our own pockets to go voyaging into this area and see if skill retrieval technologies or protocols can be developed. Want a referral for self-development work?

Other Hacking Approaches

June of 2021 my UrbanSurvival website experienced a catastrophic failure. One that lost 18-years of writing in one horrific instant.

In the process of recovering – working 50+ hours on less than 5-hours sleep in all – I went through some major self-discovery and firming of the connection to my "spirit energy." It was literally able to *power me through.*

Once the website restoration had gotten the basics back online, an inspiring email came in from a reader who was anxious to read the first part of this book. Which was presented for *Peoplenomics.com* subscribers.

I don't think he'd mind my sharing his comments:

> "Morning George,
>
> Congratulations both on Elaine's (second total hip replacement surgery - G) recovery and your progress in rebuilding your website. Perhaps the following will help you take the next large step in your life.
>
> After my folks passed away both after exceptionally long lives, I set a number of goals that I wanted to accomplish before I stepped through the last Golden Door to the other side. May 24th before the Eclipse I took the first step toward those three goals.

I joined the "IAC" the "International Academy of Consciousness" and I invested in their "CDP" the "Consciousness Development Program".
https://www.iacworld.org/attend-the-cdp/

I have been taking the online classes now for a while, working through them one by one, taking lots of notes, adjusting my own life to fit and make time to practice what I am learning. And it is now what makes me get out of bed every day with a smile on my face and I look forward to what I am learning about life on the other side, meeting souls there who have passed on, astral travel aka travel out of the body while fully awake, to the other side of life, where I'll go when I leave the physical side.

I am incredibly happy I have taken this step.

If you or others feel like that's a little extreme, may I recommend the author Luis Minero's book '"Demystifying the out-of-body Experience". A Practical Manual for Exploration and Personal Evolution'.

These tools offer a real path of exploration for all of us, regardless of beliefs.
The IAC has existed for more than 30 years. And as much as I heard such good things about Robert Monroe's Institute and had plans to attend the seminars and workshops there, I am so glad I made the choice to go with the IAC Consciousness Development Program first.

I waited till now to suggest that this is something you and Elaine will enjoy so much, being able to do together. I waited to be sure and experience and see what I would be learning and if I'd be happy with it. I wanted to bite the bullet first. Having done so, I can say that you have ask for the same tools in what you have written and what you have hunted for, for so long.

So, I hope you two follow me on my adventure and take one of your own."

For now, we're following our own path…but that's subject to change in the next, oh, three minutes. Like everything in Life can…

14. Slowing Down Aging – Mental

Although I'm sad to keep reminding you that it's a mathematical certainty (without Faith) that you will die from this physical Life, there are a number of ways to hyper-extend the life you have.

These fall into two categories: Mental, which I call "inside work" and Physical, which we'll denote as "outside work." When viewed from the perspective of inside of your eyelids.

We'll begin with a short list of what some of the "inside work" might include:

- Command and Control
- Mental Exercise
- Time use and perception
- Joy-Seeking
- Drama (and its close cousin…)
- Stress (memory management)
- Time anchors
- Earth anchors

Each one of these offers some valuable insights and strategies to *dramatically* improve your time "in the Game of Life." For this reason, such discussions can be some of the best-spent time, ever!

Command and Control

We have covered this in detail earlier, but if you've skipped ahead to this part of the book, there is some "basic ownership CLAIMING that everyone needs to accomplish. When you *own* something, you take *responsibility*. When there's no "ownership" sense, people just give themselves unwarranted "permission" to act with no accountability.

When responsibility is claimed, however, decisions are improved because the person making "the call" will consciously *own* the outcome.
I like to use the analogy that Life behaves identically to the physics law: For every *action*, there is an equal and opposite *reaction*.

When you can wake up – going an entire day *owning* that everyone single *action* of a day will result in specific proportionate *reactions* – then you are on your path to spiritual independence.

This won't inoculate you against fraudsters, liars, or spiritual miscreants; these will always be with us. But you will be able to make *better* decisions.

Life has a rule set (depending on which religion you study) has something like the rules of baseball. Where, if you want to be an All-Star, you don't have to "hit every pitch thrown" out of the park.

In fact, if you can make good "ownership of results" decisions *one-third of the time*, you will be in Hall of Fame territory. Few realize that outfielder Ty Cobb has the highest batting average in history. Batted .366 over his 24-seasons in the Majors. A little over a third of the time (.333) and he owns the category!

See how our "Game of Life" has "rules" that are pretty useful?

Mental Exercise

Another useful "rule" is "Use it or Lose it."

There are millions of ways to challenge yourself to use your brain. Most people (being average or lower) are simply too *lazy* to force themselves on toward *excellence* every waking moment. It takes extreme effort, though, so it's understandable.

Here's a short list of ways I try to keep my brain "in gear" so that I'll never be at a "loss for words" or fail to have a "template for solving" any problem I come across in life.

Remember, your list will be different. Every day, though, consider a goal of "Coming up with a shortcut to improve my human efficiency" a worthwhile endeavor. Collect problem-solving *templates*, too. This makes your problem-solving *extensible*.

- Shortcut the Weather: When you want to look up the weather in Seattle, or wherever you have family) enter it as a Zip Code in AccuWeather or WeatherUnderground. Three reasons to do this:

First reason is it's *faster*. Unless you live in a three-letter city in a two-letter state. Second, it *exercises* your *recall function*. Third is it *expands* your "domain of thinking" into numerical – not simply alphabetical – contexts.

My children's weather Zip codes are 98406, 98004, 98034, and 98826. Our little hangout in the woods is 75803.

As an alternative? Use airport codes. KTIW, KSEA, KEAT, and KPSN will get me in the ballpark.

Better? Zip codes on even days, nearby airports on odd days.

- Use a Foreign Language: People – says the data – often have a "senior language learning window." Somewhere over age 50-60 it actually becomes easier to learn a whole new language than add layers of knowledge in your native tongue. We could have a geeky computer discussion here that would go: It's faster for a single processor to search two or three smaller databases than it is to search a single *large* database.

My "foreign language" is Morse code at reasonably high speeds (25-40 words per minute). This is not just a translation exercise, but a speed test as well. Since most languages are pretty stable in the 100-150 word per minute range. Faster in big cities, slower in the country; noticeably. High speed Morse has one feature spoken language does not: In event of a stroke, wife Elaine knows I will still be able to "get in formation out of my head" using code. Might be something as small as a finger twitch, but if I'm awake, comms will be up.

- Use a Comprehensive Worldview. We already
  talked about how all you need do to improve recall
  is *grant yourself permission* to have a perfect
  memory. But it helps (in a "mental castle"
  memory system way) to have a comprehensive grid
  system where you can store concepts.

I use a "Seven Major Systems of Life" technique: Food &
Water, Shelter, Communications, Transportation, Energy,
Environment, and Finance. Every time "new information"
comes along, take a moment to appreciate its *systemic
relationships*. When done, conceptualization is much faster.

Each of these "major systems" has its own embedded
hierarchy. Protein, grain, dairy, fruits, and veggies for the
Food system, for example. And all systems intersect with all
others.

Example? Sure: consider the Transportation hierarchy, which
is ground, air, and water, the intersecting with Food
(subheading Vegetables) could describe the snack counter at
the airport. Transportation (water) intersects with Food:
protein at the local fish and chips joint, to carry it out a bit.

Transportation subhead Air intersects with these big Housing
units called hangars...seeing how this works?

- Playback Great Performances. Because your brain
  really does record *everything* arriving from your
  tactile senses (sight, sound, touch, smell, taste –
  and even *intuition*), take a moment once a day to
  mentally "play back" something you experienced
  earlier in the day. As you get better, play back

importance scenes from yesterday, last week, and so on. The information is there. You just haven't pushed yourself to dig into it.

- One of my favorite music tracks to play back is the *Charles Lloyd Quartet* recording of *Forest Flower Sunrise, Forest Flower Sunset* recorded live at the Monterey Jazz Festival in 1965 or 66. Interesting mental challenge (particularly the passage in this live recording where the small plane flew over.). Just four musical instruments, ambient crowd noise, and a single-engine plane over about 18-minutes of locked-in the mental suitcase experience. Not difficult and very pleasing. Oh-oh…did I just let one out, again?

Another Big Secret in this Book:

People don't really need a Sony *Walkman* – or a radio, either - unless the information has extreme time value. Like a ball game or current weather. It's just that a digital audio player is a lot more convenient than using the brain. Especially if you're trying to adjust audio compression, equalization, and room acoustics inside that "Concert Hall Between Your Ears." Sure, I find it's more accurate to use a pair of dBX T-160A compressor-limiters in our home studio, no doubt.

This little secret, though, should never be overlooked because it's why many people (with skills like sound, speech, and concert-level playback using just their minds) can tolerate almost unlimited isolation from other people. There is *so damn much resource between your ears – besides the suitcase! Concert hall, library, photo collection and even video clips galore!*

Oh, and yeah, did we mention in the mental concert hall between the ears, you can play back at will 24/7 – any volume desired - without waking anyone else up? I can't tell you how many times I've played cinematic John Williams and BSO tracks in my head getting back to sleep at 2:30AM. Elaine never heard a peep. See how useful this is?

Key Takeaway: This should give you an idea how vastly larger our suitcase filling project is!

Ham Sandwich and Beer bet says most ADHD people already know this but have had a very difficult time trying to articulate this to the pure linear thinkers.

Think Faster – Live Longer

It might be argued that all my attention to various forms of high-speed mental fitness is without reason. After all, you have a *Walkman* and the .MP3 collection, so why tie up the mental processor, right?

Which gets us back to the realization point: When we *DIE* the *Walkman* isn't going to work in the grave.

The other thing developing prodigious recall will do is that if will make you live perhaps *twice as long.*

Here's how – in simple to understand computer terms.

Consider an average brain like an early computer processor. An old *Intel* 8080 was really good at keeping a wort processor working. But nothing beats the current model I9 (or multi-core *Xeon*) series processors when comes to high-end multi-channel media production.

One processor was slow (8080) and one screaming so fast that liquid cooling might be desired. The earlier processor might print a <u>page</u> per second. Newest? It's up in <u>books</u> *per second.* With enough cores and DDR4 RAM? *Hours of video with Surround Sound per second.*

To bring this around: If you don't constantly push yourself, you may be "technically" alive and all. But you're doing life at one *page per second.* Work on upgrading the performance of your onboard processor and suddenly you can assimilate (and take with you into whatever follows Death) two to *one hundred times or more.*

The implication? Working the brain may be one effective strategy toward skipping repeated reincarnations. Why live 100 different lives when you can get 200X out of a single – *well optimized* – Life?

Paradox of Joy-Seeking

Now that we have a whole strategy to put more into the Suitcase Between Your Ears, see what has changed?

The *nature of Joy-Seeking* changes.

A successful life is the successive realization of progressively more worthwhile goals.

At age 21, my idea of joy-seeking was a gorgeous partner of the opposite sex, a fine meal, and refining basic reproductive skills and mutual pleasuring. Don't misunderstand… that still works in our 70s!

But the *breadth* of joy changes. Moneymaking tried to catch up with sex. Attaining goals like a first home, first marriage, and so forth figure in, too.

Somewhere in mid-life, after the second divorce, I realized my focus on Joy had changed when I began to *troubleshootize* major aspects of pleasure.

This was the period when I confirmed that one great step toward a perfect relationship was "M.F.M.B." Matching Food Means Matching Breath.

See, there were times my partner would not seem *as appealing*. I couldn't for the life of me figure out why. All the "technical checkboxes were right."

Then it hit me: Smell of garlic. Since I hadn't had any, odor was like being smacked by a runaway freight train – from Italy.

By then, I had read the definitive book on the Russia science of invention, TRIZ. Which is short for "teoriya resheniya izobretatelskikh zadatch, literally: "theory of the resolution of invention-related tasks") is "a problem-solving, analysis and forecasting tool derived from the study of patterns of invention in the global patent literature".

The book *And Suddenly the Inventor Appeared"* and the newly minted distance-learning MBA were two fundamental changes in joy-seeking I wish had achieved half a century earlier in Life.

TRIZ is essentially a list of 38 to 40 ways you can *physically change things* in your world. Make them bigger, smaller, rounder, squarer, freeze them, burn them, change their chemistry, and so forth. Systematic invention, got it?

All I had to do was ensure that when dating, I'd eat *exactly* the same food as the person I was with. See, over time chemistry works the same. When you and a partner are breaking down similar food, your chemical reactions will be similar – and with it, the off-gassing.

Life Optimizing Got Serious

Following my second divorce and having conquered the "differences in body chemistry" issue, I started looking past sex, bank account numbers, and a whole lot of other "marketed to us" values that we simply accept and act on. With really very little retrospection or critical thought.

As a result, Joy-Seeking evolved. I had enjoyed flying a light plane when younger (early stages of marriage #2) but that was shelved due to financial commitments and home ownership. By 2000, though, I was an optimizing sonovabitch.

Found the safest and best way to reactivate my pilot's license. Bought a plane. And now married (to an equal believer in MFMB) we flew all over the country in our plane.

Then the adversity of a dislocated interocular lens implant resulted in eye surgeries. While I would still be able to fly with hard contacts, the idea of losing a contact on "short final" was another easy to solve optimization. There'd be no do-overs from a very bad landing.

But somehow, one set of optimizations falling resulted in another one rising: Working in the shop and studying of *Walt Disney Imagineering*™ opened the door to a "movie set house." Elaine articulates it best: A home that *transports* us. Which has led to our shared "laugh at life" a home with a major personality for every room. Like *movie set* transporting. Not putting up a "boat picture" and calling a room "nautically themed."

Since life began to "settle into its path" following Divorce #2, a vague outline of a pattern has emerged. People seem to be capable of god-like (or goddess-like) realization of "neat stuff" when they mix equal parts of physical skills, imagination, and learning.

Nice thing about "packing to die" is that you no longer need to justify (or excuse) behaviors that border on irrational. It is only "crazy" for a 70-something to pick up some schooling in "tiny machine language" if you insist that like most tech, TinyML will only be a subject for 50-100 years. After which it will be *else*.

The current reading list looks like a Dewey Decimal dart contest. Yet, it's how people really work. They get to new places by reconnecting with old ones in new and novel ways.

Place and Time Anchors

Our cobbling a home into something else (back-to-back movie sets?) underscores another Death delaying tactic. It forces us to never be in exactly the "same place" and thus, an old story comes to mind. It was retold by W. Somerset Maugham in 1933.

(The story is told by Death speaking the part:)

> "There was a merchant in Bagdad who sent his servant to market to buy provisions and in a little while the servant came back, white and trembling, and said, Master, just now when I was in the marketplace I was jostled by a woman in the crowd and when I turned, I saw it was Death that jostled me. She looked at me and made a threatening gesture, now, lend me your horse, and I will ride away from this city and avoid my fate. I will go to Samarra and there, Death will not find me.
>
> The merchant lent him his horse, and the servant mounted it, and he dug his spurs in its flanks and as fast as the horse could gallop, he went. Then the merchant went down to the marketplace, and he saw me standing in the crowd and he came to me (Death) and said, "Why did you make a threating gesture to my servant when you saw him this morning?"

"That was not a threatening gesture," I (Death) said, "It was only a start of surprise. I was astonished to see him in Bagdad, for I had an appointment with him tonight in Samarra."

What Maugham gets to, runs deep in all of us, to one extent, or another. We all want to "out-run" Death.

Our thinking (such as it is) holds that by *continually reinventing ourselves*, we will not be so recognizable as the Servant in the story. Thus, through a conscious effort of continual renewal and reinvention, we not only *might* trick death for a few seconds, but something more important. We fully live each moment of Life.

Time Anchors

Some people run from death's inevitability using what I call "Time Anchors." A variant can be thought of as "Place Anchors."

The way a Time Anchor works is when people mentally *regress themselves* to an earlier period of their Life. One where they were younger, prettier, more vivacious, more clever, wittier, and of course, wrinkle-free. Usually, though, people just look absurd.

This doesn't mean Time Anchors don't work: Wife Elaine still fits into clothes she has owned since high school. The reason she can "pull it off" (wearing clothes of a 25-year-old disco diva) is that is *who she really is*. That being *solidly anchored to an optimum everything in her life* is what (for her) keeps death at bay.

The non-functioning Time Anchor attempt is when a person over 70 tries to *act* like something <u>they are not.</u> In which case, the time anchor is false (a kind of denial) and failing to have congruence between bespoke and actual appearances can merely *increase stress.*

In Elaine's case, her healing time from her second total hip replacement was damn near miraculous: About what would be expected from a 25-year-old. Less than two months. See, when your mental age permeates your *whole being* then the old saying "We're always the same age on the *inside*" becomes true.

For most people, it's not. They have aged in the brain. They no longer seek the most modern music, keep up on fashion, have an eye for what's *sexy* and so forth. As a result when they try to "act young" it's only a charade. Not a full meal deal.

Stress Kills

This gets us to one of the most important aspects of living a long life. Stress elimination.

You can't ever eliminate *all* stress. Besides, a little stress (positive stress) can be good for us.

How about starting with the simplest definition of stress I've found:

> "Stress is the difference between who or where or what you CLAIM as opposed to what, where, or who REALLY are."

Going back to Elaine's time anchor period (disco diva), while she would likely admit (depending on how well she knows you) to her disco days, there is no *stress* because that genuinely is who she IS – even now.

She has a delightfully grounded way of blowing-off almost anything bad that has ever happened and refusing to allow that into her thinking. It's actually a form of "practiced forgetting." Over time, she's gotten very good at it. And as a result, she is very "low stress." She gets mad, sometimes, like anyone else. Yet, like a passing thunderstorm, never seen it last more than an hour, or two.

Now, let's look at the other end of the spectrum. A somewhat obscure book in the collection is "The Mind and Cancer" by Tom Laughlin and Dr. James P. Morgan. In which six psychological traits of cancer victims are explored. A lot of these have to do with (generally) repression. Holding back anger, holding back emotions, and so forth. Rather than getting mad and getting on…

When young, it's easy to have a *ton* of stress onboarded by the constant barrage of information we're all subjected to. But, for the most part, the thing that helps people with any fatal disease most (including Life itself) is to *not stress over it.*

Even though it's inevitable? And more people than ever before are around who ABSOLUTELY will die? Mass media is firmly in the role of "Denial Enabler" telling us we must behave in this way or buy that.

Finest stress management book ever? I'd nominate Mark Manson's book: "The Subtle Art of Not Giving a F*ck: A Counterintuitive Approach to Living a Good Life." Haven't we talked about how that other big secret works? *Getting Over It.*

Negative stress really does kill. While we all have an appointment in Samarra, between now and then? F*ck it…let's move on. If we don't, dwelling becomes the slow-motion killing of ourselves.

Avoid stress and realize that there are a lot of people who will try to bring their drama into your life. Send them away, directly. Drama begets stress. Stress makes phone calls to Life's front desk and tries to move up your scheduled check-out time.

Hide the electronics – and you hide the drama. This reduces stress.

15. Slowing Physical Aging (Basics)

Knowing a bit more about Death changes things up in your life. *"If I only had more time to prepare…"* kind of thing.

Even if you have an unstoppable powerhouse of a brain going for you. It's time – if you haven't done this yet – to "throw some chemistry at the problem." Because the old childhood reminder (*"You are what you eat."*) gets *truer* with each passing year until we "climb in the box." The blocking and tackling of Death starts at the breakfast table and rages until the last snack before bed.

Our starting points for this chapter include the following data discussions:

- Your Aging environment
- Physical risk avoidance
- Breathe deep
- Move, damn it
- Sleep time adventures
- Location, location
- Water: Plain and structured
- Light: Plain and planned
- Eating well

This is a huge amount of material, but if we take it one step at a time, there is a flow to it. Framework, flow.

Controlling Your Environment

Assuming you are serious about postponing the arrival of Death, how serious are you about accomplishing the task? Because I'll tell you right now, most people are *not*. Lots of talkers, few walkers.

Few sit down and take widely available facts (everyone's got the Internet), assemble them into "optimization lists" and from these derive "tasking operations" to achieve the benefits.

Of course, no one's will be perfect. Beating a few minutes back from the grasp of Death may only result in a short delay of our trips to Samarra.

Still, as a "raging against the falling night" species, getting aggressively proactive beats the hell out of couch-riding reruns into the Great Beyond. Unless you haven't had enough of commercials…

Physical Risk Avoidance

Let's assume you are smart enough *not* to step in front of a bus. More to point, you will lock your doors (even during the day). You have 9-1-1 on the speed dial and a small armory in the top drawer of your nightstand next to the bed.

There's also a smoke detector and a secondary carbon monoxide detector, a first aid kit, regular health checkups and all that sort of stuff.

A lot of people miss extending risk reduction just a little further. For example, we have half a dozen dry chemical fire extinguishers handy, a bottle of oxygen, plus assorted other tools and supplies for a "worst case" event.

But there's a big one which is called AARP. No, silly, not the *retirement newsletter and insurance outfit!* Age Adjusted Risk Prevention.

You can find a number of online services that will give you a reasonable sense of your reaction speed. This stretches out as you age. When you are in your upper teens to mid-20s? Those reaction times may be in the 300-millisecond range. But, by age 67, for example, the average reaction as slowed to 771-milliseconds. This morning I was testing in the mid-50s which is better than the expected for age 72 which is more likely to be in the range of 819-milliseconds.

You can find a number of such tests online. I like the *JustPark.com* creative reaction time tester (Google it).

There are some caveats: When tracking your reaction time, remember to do both right-hand and left-hand reaction speeds. Your brain has two halves to it, and a change in reaction speed of more than a few hundred milliseconds might be worth mentioning to your doctor. Strokes and mini strokes come to mind.

A second speed bump here is? Doing enough speed tests that your reactions become "automatic." In other words, routine to the point of passing reactions around the conscious brain. When this occurs, you're doing some "neural pathing" (good) but you're also lying to yourself if you base higher level physical tasks on automated reaction speeds. Reason is a deer isn't jumping out of the woods into the grill of your car 4-times per minute. Life is a lot less predictable than that.

When used, the reaction speed tests, averaged for both sides of the brain (600.7 milliseconds for this morning's run here) should be considered against the task under consideration. Since 600 ms. is likely OK for climbing a ladder, have fun up on the roof. But if you look at demographics of falls when the average creeps up to the 700 ms. age range, a number of activities might come off the table.

In order, the age and time the activities were set aside began with selling my Yamaha *Virago* 650-shaft drive motorcycle. Sweet ride, but a cousin (a bit younger) lost a foot in a bike accident, and I was about to be a parent. A look at accident statistics suggested some wisdom in taking the helmet off at age 28.

Serious sailing, including a whiff of offshore (coastwise) came to a screeching halt at age 55. While this was largely due to a shift of employment that left our sailboat moored in San Diego while I was "softwaring" in Florida, the world had changed after 2001, Twin Towers and all: the future of vagabond liveaboard sailing became sketchy.

A succession of fast cars passed through our lives. Elaine was a *Corvette* driver. Me? Still a recovering *Porsche 930* driver. When we hit our 60s, the superb service, ride, and performance mix of a Lexus became a "deal we couldn't say no to."

The displacement of an intraocular lens in my left eye
dropped vision down to 20-35. Which is at the upper end of
unrestricted driving. There went the Beechcraft. Sold in 2018
my reaction speeds were dropping out of the upper 20-year to
mid-30-year-old range. Sometimes, you just have to adapt,
improvise, and overcome.

It's not like there isn't always *something* neat to do in Life. We
have "fade capable hobbies" lined up all over the place here.
To be sure, learning surface mount device soldering took an
LED microscope (plus a USB plug-in camera). But with 600+
books on our *Kindles* where the font size can be upscaled, we
should be in learning mode right down to 'nails-in' time.

Breathe Deep

Had a touch of asthma my whole life. Bit more, actually, if
you count a few trips to the hospital as a child turning blue.
That's enough to warrant a discussion of breathing – because
lung deficiencies with the *'Rona* plus COPD are becoming
more common – the *real* reason to breathe is cancer.

Don't know how much you have read on hyperbaric (oxygen
saturation under modest pressure), but it has many adherents
who have beaten-back cancer. The data – starting with the
Otto Warburg work in the 1930's and progressing to a 3-way
Nobel Prize in 2019 for how cells react to (and sense) oxygen –
makes the case that deep breathing is a worthwhile daily
checklist item.

My personal experience with deep breathing goes back to summer afternoons when my buddy (*the Major*) and I would stand on a steep slope in the front yard and hyperventilate like crazy for a few seconds. Age 10? Then, holding our breath, we'd gently fall back onto the soft grass.

I skip the "knockout" part now but hyperventilating a few times a day when you remember (and breathing less deeply when the stars begin) may not be a bad thing. In Asian and Indian religions, such working of "prana" and "mindful breathing" is key to enlightenment. We'll skip that (we're doing a movie, right?) but it probably won't hurt, either.

Move, Damn It

Every day – or every *other* at minimum – I try to get the heart rate up to something interesting. There's a simple way to figure your age-adjusted [maximum] level: Take the number **220** *and subtract your Age*.

Assuming I am 73, my <u>maximum</u> number is 220 minus 73 which gives an exercise heart rate of 147. For cardio work, the target range is 70 to 80 percent of that. Call it 118 on the high end. On our treadmill, it settles out around 100 with a good walk. 120 if brisk.

There's much debate about short-term high intensity training (SHIT, lol). One school of thought says do all your exercise at once and then relax. Others say there's more benefit breaking it into 2 to 4 sessions per day. I'll toss that research problem in your lap.

And do talk to your doctor in advance. Prescriptions and general condition may change the guidance. Amazing, though, what great condition some of the old farmers out here in East Texas are in. Toss bales all day. Puts the software-damaged youth to shame. Couch disease.

Sleep Time Adventure

There is a "sweet spot" for sleep. The Centers for Disease Control offers a table view:

Age Group		Recommended Hours of Sleep Per Day
Newborn	0–3 months	14–17 hours (National Sleep Foundation)[1] No recommendation (American Academy of Sleep Medicine)[2]
Infant	4–12 months	12–16 hours per 24 hours (including naps)[2]
Toddler	1–2 years	11–14 hours per 24 hours (including naps)[2]
Preschool	3–5 years	10–13 hours per 24 hours (including naps)[2]
School Age	6–12 years	9–12 hours per 24 hours[2]
Teen	13–18 years	8–10 hours per 24 hours[2]
Adult	18–60 years	7 or more hours per night[3]
	61–64 years	7–9 hours[1]
	65 years and older	7–8 hours[1]

Since I only got 5 to 8-hours of sleep as a teen, staying up all night working on electronics oftentimes, maybe we OCD types were sleep-deprived? This was back when riding a bicycle 40-miles a day was no big deal. In hilly country, too. Burning both ends *weren't no big deal*! Today? Seems to be increasingly difficult.

Location, Location

You might not (conventionally) think of where you live as being a major factor in living a good, strong, long life, but it may be.

One reason can be weather: If you're in Minnesota, slipping and falling on ice is an annual winter threat. In Florida? Not so much. Hawaii? Stay down from Haleakala and you'll have no trouble.

Other life extending factors include the local water supplies, air quality and pollution levels, plus social density pressures. Don't step in front of a bus, though.

This population density question is interesting: Being around a lot of people *used* to be fun. Since the *'Rona* not so much.

People – even neighbors – can be a real source of stress. Especially if they have contracted PCD (political-correctness disease). On the other hand, there's no such thing as "*3-minute drop to shock*" times in rural medicine. When a neighbor of ours died (running over an extension cord on a riding mower and trying to untangle it with the plug still in…) the response time was right at 18-minutes.

Urban, rural, or somewhere in between is a difficult choice matrix.

Cities have incredibly high property taxes. A modest home we looked at in Tyler, Texas (pool, greenhouse, $475K) was under consideration until I looked at the property taxes: $7,800 a year. That's effectively $650 per month to *rent your home back from the government.* Pass!

Our original selection (curtain #2?) was extremely rural on a tree farm. 29-acres and only $600 a year in property taxes. Double-wide mobile home, big shop.

Here's how it tallied: Dead from slow medical response? Or, be taxed to death which is a whole *other* level of stress and dependence on government. Thanks, we're a little too independent to run through that cattle chute.

Main thing to keep in mind is where your genetic ancestry is *from.* Pick conditions as close to your average ancestors back 5-10 generations if you can sort it out.

Haven't seen much work on this, but humans are loosely optimized by our genetics - over time - for a certain kind of natural setting. Elaine and me? Northern Europeans. So, we eat accordingly, and eschew extremes of cold and heat. Texas outside the hell months of summer is surprisingly mild.

From the Mediterranean countries? Consider a state like California (southern). From China? Depends on family tree because of the vast climate range in China. Africa? Warmer parts of the country might fit along with warm weather fruits and vegetables. Maybe less fish, more fowl. The "privilege" of a northern Euro pool is more celery, cabbage, carrots, and onions. More fish and lots of pork. Eat what agrees with you.

All you need to do is look where your family genes came from (Scotland, Denmark, and Sweden with a dash of England for us) and eat accordingly. Though I really don't like oatmeal! Scotch whiskey is an endearing offset. High in iodine, too, from the peat lands.

Water: Plain and Structured

What's water? "Oh, the *wet stuff*?"

Well, obviously, you have never done much hydroponic gardening. Water can run from mildly acidic (a pH of 7.2 is common in the Pacific Northwest), to quite alkaline. Our local water runs a pH of 8.3 in the summer which makes hydroponics more a massive home chemistry set than source of "organic" food.

Structured water is a different thing: The idea is that water not only has some basic chemistry to it, but that when agitated (in a blender for 30-seconds and cool to cold) the water changes at a molecular level.

You will want to read "The Fourth Phase of Water" by Gerald H. Pollock. His basic premise is water has not been adequately studied. It has both liquid features, but depending on how it's treated, there are also properties of *gels* and there are *liquid crystalline* structures, as well.

Sure, sounds like New Age crackpot bullshit, until you check his creds on his Amazon author page. Does this sound like a loon, to you?

"2012 recipient of the coveted Prigogine Medal for thermodynamics of dissipative systems. He has received an honorary doctorate from Ural State University in Ekaterinburg, Russia, and was more recently named an Honorary Professor of the Russian Academy of Sciences, and Foreign Member of the Srpska Academy. Pollack is a Founding Fellow of the American Institute of Medical and Biological Engineering and a Fellow of both the American Heart Association and the Biomedical Engineering Society. He recently received an NIH Director's Transformative R01 Award for his work on water and maintains an active laboratory in Seattle."

Since we don't *know* with precision exactly how much agitation is "enough" to get health benefits, even a 30-second run with a hand blender likely improves on "raw hydration" effects of water, but more importantly, the underlying *functionality* of the water.

Since you're a grown up, no more fluoride than naturally occurring unless you live in a fluoride-deficient region. Medical content advice on many elements might distill to MED – short for *minimum effective dose.*

Same with chlorine and bromines that are used for water purification. If we were 20-years younger? We'd likely spring for a whole-house reverse osmosis filtration system with UV light treatment. That would bring down the high pH, but some naturally occurring magnesium may not be bad.

The CDC in "Water-related Diseases and Contaminants in Public Water Systems" notes that *e. coli* bacteria is the 10th most common water-borne disease in America. Thing is? It's in a tie with *excess fluoride!*

Deeply reading your water supply company (or agency) annual water quality report is highly recommended. You are what you eat, but since your body is 70% water (round number) water is at least twice as important as food…

We would also recommend you study the concentrations of lithium in public drinking water and pay particularly close attention to states with almost no lithium in the water. Like Washington state. Then, look at a map of highest Alzheimer's rates in the country (like Washington state). Figure out for yourself if there's a correlation.

Same thing with dementia: Obvious when you hit disease maps that show the rates of dementia are highest in states with high latitudes. Low vitamin D levels seem to be correlated with dementia occurrence. Which explains why we have never been in a hurry to move north from Texas. Best dementia risks seem to be Florida (lithium and sun, but even useable beaches in summer). While some southern states (Texas) just get too damn hot. So, despite good lithium levels, people turn on the a/c and head indoors."

Light: Plain and Planned

Topic near and dear to us. The benefits of "plain light" are numerous. Mood and awakening of bright daylight. Red night to slow circadian rhythms when getting ready for sleep. Then there's direct whole-body light from sun to create melatonin and vitamin D which hardly anyone gets enough of…

Structured light which we also use is applied in two forms. A "light crown" of 300 LED emitters at 660 nm and longer which may provide transcranial stimulation and help repair the brain. Also being tested to help with everything from Alzheimer's to baldness. A search of PubMed.gov and ClinicalTrials.gov for low level laser light therapy (LLLLT or simply LLT) and photobiomodulation will get you a gold mine.

Stop Eating Sugars, Be Statin Skeptical

There is a strong link between aging and sugar. Not just cane, but fructose (fruit sugar) as well.

For one thing (and looks *do* matter in our world), sugar in the bloodstream tends to break down collagen. Because of how sugar contributes to both wrinkles and skin dysfunction; some even notice a link between high sugar use and dark circles under the eyes.

If that's not enough? High amounts of sugar have been shown to be statistically linked to certain kinds of cancers. While the relationship seems quite non-linear (and varies widely on family genetics) the data says leave it alone. Semi-sweet fruits (like pineapple) may be better for you than super-sweet hybrid melons, for example. A Google search "Link between sugar and aging" will turn up a ton of starting points for your further study.

Additional risks of sugar? Higher levels of inflammation, increased risk of fatty liver disease, and decreases in the immune system.

One reason, we think, that Elaine looks as much as 30-years younger than her birth certificate age is that years ago, she read the Patrick Duffy book *"Sugar Blues."* Published in 1975, the Duffy book (still available via *Amazon*) is a real indictment of sugar.

On my *UrbanSurvival.com* and *Peoplenomics.com* websites, I often cite a way of looking at many public policy issues along with product marketing as means to *maximize cash flows and profits* of major corporations. The increased marketing of sugars in the 1960s and 70s brought us a cornucopia of sugary breakfast foods and addictive caffeinated soft drinks. Really tasty, for sure. Really good for public health? Not so much.

A similar *monetization of health* is seen in a couple of other good books – this time having to do with the national disaster in cardiovascular health.

You see, a lot of people began (what pilots would call *their initial descent*) into compromised health way back in the 1950s. When *hydrogenated oils* were brought to market as butter replacements.

The pioneering work on this was published in *"The Oiling of America"* (1998, Eng and Fallon) and went through the evolution of vegetable-based hydrogenation leading to cardiovascular issues. For example:

"A 1955 report on artery plaques in soldiers killed during the Korean War showed little difference in the number and severity of plaques between American soldiers and those of Japanese natives - 75 per cent versus 65 per cent - even though the Japanese diet at the time was lower in animal products and fat. A 1957 study of the largely vegetarian Bantu found that they had as much atheroma - occlusions or plaque build-up in the arteries - as other races from South Africa who ate more meat. A 1958 report noted that Jamaican Blacks showed a degree of atherosclerosis comparable to that found in the United States, although they suffered from lower rates of heart disease. A 1960 report noted that the severity of atherosclerotic lesions in Japan approached that of the United States."

As their work progressed, the book (and 2008 video) piled on the facts:

"The 1968 International Atherosclerosis Project, in which over 22,000 corpses in 14 nations were cut open and examined for plaques in the arteries, showed the same degree of atheroma in all parts of the world - in populations that suffered from a great deal of heart disease, and in populations that had very little or none at all."

An old Mark Twain saying, words to the effect that *"Lies spread halfway around the world before the truth has even gotten out of bed in the morning"* seems to hold true, or partly so, in medicine.

But monetizations?

Medicine seized on the idea that serum cholesterol level management was the "be-all, end-all" and along came lipid management as a billion-dollar (now even larger) industry.

Statins (with double entendre names live "lovastatin") hit the market with perks to cooperating early adopting doctors. Who wouldn't "love-a-statin" that was printing millions in profits?

Yet even now, a quiet – data based – backlash has begun.

One of the earliest books that opened my eyes came in 2012 when I decided to read "Ignore the awkward! How the cholesterol myths are kept alive" *Kindle* Edition, by Uffe Ravnskov.

Among other things, this book explained that many of the claimed "cholesterol lowering benefits" seen in the *Naples Study* didn't really come from eating the lower cholesterol diet (which was then evolved into medium-chain-triglyceride heavy eating plans). No, said author Uffe Ravnskov: Lower cholesterol was shown because so many people in the Naples region were on the verge of starvation in the wake of screwed up food distribution systems following World War 2. Initially claimed as low fat by one Ancel Keys.

NPR did a story in 2011 admitting "Mediterraneans abandon their famous diet." Not surprisingly, at least to researchers like Uffe Ravnskov, there's a much simpler answer. And yes, Occam's Razor is still sharp:

When the human body is low on nutrition, the serum lipid levels drop. Since serum lipids have everything to do with inflammation (via such causes as high serum uric acid levels) diseases like gout (a form of arthritis) are also reduced. Pain eases on the Med Diet.

The medical question, thus became clear: Was there a lot to be gained from a *semi-calorie restricted diet* rather than a statin monetization program? Don't worry! The answer is Big Money always wins.

So do color us skeptical on the data.

My own trial experience, though, is what "sealed the deal" (no statins, no way) for me occurred about five or six years ago. At the urging of my PCP, I began statins and stayed on them religiously for all of three weeks.

At the end of my onboarding effort, I had all the symptoms of statins not working as advertised: I experienced muscle pain, cramps, nausea, and headaches. Within 3-days of getting rid of the statins, I was feeling "in the pink" again.

This, and having done some basic *kinesiology* work with a well-degreed subtle energy researcher years ago, I came to a personal belief that the best way to manage health issues for your body is to simply sit back, relax, and sense what your body is telling you.

If something makes you feel bad – and is sold as a long-term solution – you have every right to be skeptical. Short-term pain is one thing (Elaine's hip replacement recovery is an example, or a friend's experience with successful chemotherapy). But long-term effects?

I'll pass. You get to make your own (informed) healthcare decisions. But at every step of the way, I now aggressively engage with my Primary Care Physician (PCP):

- By asking what best practices are.

- By demanding solid data.
- By doing my own thorough research using medically competent sources, including and especially specialty journal cites on PubMed.gov.
- By using only solutions that have been through rigorous (and complete!) clinical trials.
- And then listening clearly and critically to my body's feedback.

This is NOT advice. But it works for me. When I feel sluggish, a day, or less, without food seems to "pop me back into shape."

So does a look for environmental causes. Dehydration? Too many martinis previous day? Not enough exercise? Too much? Been around sick people?

A friend of ours has MS. While conventional medicine says there are four classes of causation, a single source isn't clear (Infection, genetics, immune system, and environment). Yet doctors don't usually "empower patients" to become their "active research partners."

If they did, there would be a worksheet on different vitamin and mineral supplements to try. And solutions that are unlikely to even rise to the investigation level in medicine, such as trying C60 fullerenes, or a calorie-restricted diet, or removing certain nutrients. Change just doesn't happen fast enough.

At least, not in our view.

Eating Well

Everyone knows the basics here: Eat the five food groups every day. *(We add wine as a food group.) What makes you feel good – inside and out - really matters.

Eat in moderation and really important, eat simply. This means a minimum of "convenience foods" because those have all kinds of flavor and texture "enhancers" that humans were never genetically designed to process.

"Mom, can I have another helping of artificially flavored texturized vegetable protein with extra high-fructose corn syrup and extra BHA and preservatives, please?" Hmm…can't say as I recall Mom ever OK'ing that…

During my single years, a good meal was a couple of martinis, a slab of steak (medium rare) and a tossed salad. Still think that. There's a wonderful book you can find on the web (free, see the *A. Weston Price Foundation* website) called the "Oiling of America." It's all about how a good portion of the cholesterol epidemic is due to hydrogenated fats passed off as "healthy." They are not.

In a family that was of Northern European descent, we ate butter all the time. Real stuff. Back when the news about dangers of hydrogenated oils began to leak out in the early 1960s. Hasn't seemed to have had much impact. Mom hit 93 before taking up her suitcase.

The best food is the freshest, which is why we strongly advocate even a small home garden plot. The notion of a 3,000-mile supply line for food is a waste of resources and undermines the whole notion of food as a basic human right. If you can grow it where you live, it's probably better than anything from the store not fresh and locally sourced. Except peanuts, of course, to those with allergies.

A not so funny thing happens to some seniors: They tend to get "backed-up" at times. The literature says there are often several easy to resolve alternatives. Stool softeners are not on our list. Drinking more water, adding more veggies, especially those high in fiber and super-especially the ones harder to break down (corn on the cob?) can help. When all else fails, two or three glasses of red wine before a dinner of a fatty meat (rib steak), tossed salad, corn on the cob. Four grams of Vitamin C?

And think about sleeping on a towel.

Two cups of strong coffee when you first get up often has a similar effect to a couple of sticks of dynamite in all but the most extreme cases.

If you're still backed up? (Check to see if you're a politician and your head is in the way...) Repeat again but now we're edging toward primary care physician country.

16. Advanced Anti-Aging

Having done the "basics" (good water, sleep, food, breathing, exercise) you'd think that ought to be enough. But, to ensure you can get through the "Packing to Die Process" still ahead in this book, there are additional steps to be studied.

Here's the hit list:

- Frontline Defenses
    - Vaccinations matter - but there's choice, too
    - Bugs, Nootropics, and *Nature*
- Physical Concepts
    - Telomeres, methylation, and oxidation
    - Hydration
    - Food and Supplementation
- Two Stacks, Two levers
    - Morning stack
    - Evening stack
    - Brain levers (coffee, drugs, and alcohol)
- A Well Scheduled Life

Frontline Defenses

The *Pareto Principle* instructs us that 80 percent of our results will come from 20 percent of our actions. It's an easy thumbnail to remember, but when applied to aging it's a sonovabitch.

My father passed on (82, Alzheimer's) after a good run. Mom hit 93. So, I reckon a good target for me (doing *mostly* what they did would be the midpoint: about 87.

Thing is *Pareto* hints that a lot of our parents were only able to do about 80%. They didn't have "3-minute drop to shock" EMT service. The food was generally fresher and less processed. But there were additives, especially in cereal packaging and such. RBST-free milk wasn't around.

At age 65, though, it dawned on me that 80 percent of my target age (87) was only 72. *Ye gods!* That's *right now.*

It was more than enough to kick-start me on an improved lifestyle. Alcohol intake declined. Work around our homestead increased. I tried to get real work done and not waste it on a machine, though we have a treadmill, weight machine, inclined board, free weights, a kettle ball or two, plus bands, along with… Well, you have the idea.

Vaccinations? Yes but there's Choice

"This Does Not Constitute Medical Advice." Readers need to consult with their PCPs on the best way to handle vaccination choices.

Like many other tasks, the answer to the questions about aging seemed to arise through study of the data.

I haven't had a lot of vaccinations in my life; polio as a kid, a tetanus shot for a an early 20s fall with a sharp power saw, and an IV of propanol for a couple of eye surgeries and a navel hernia mesh implant. Overall, pretty healthy, though.

Then I started to look at the stats. One of the biggest causes of death for seniors was pneumonia. The more I looked at the coincident disease that really delivers the knock-out punch, even with things like a respiratory infection and Covid, the fatal blows seemed to come from pneumonia.

The two-part pneumonia shot for Elaine and me was a no-brainer.

The Covid-19 virus was a different calculation, though. As of press time, we are still considering our options and not taking the vax, yet. My read of the data says that the mRNA "vaccines" were all built from computer estimations of what ought to make the body produce an antigen to the coronavirus spike protein. It was not *grown from a sample.* It's an estimation. A toxin.

That took the two mRNA approaches off the table: Pfizer and Moderna. This left Johnson & Johnson (DNA. Not an mRNA toxin) and Novavax which a friend of ours recommended after being in the trials for that.

The difficulty we have with the mRNA vaccines is they seem
to have left little defense from variants. While we wait for
data to evolve, Elaine and I have become hermit-like in our
behavior. Our contact with the world is electronic mostly.

Odd trips to the store are to have groceries ordered online
thrown into the trunk of the car and to glove-up and mask-up
(N95 or N100) because we see little (if any) benefit to cloth
masks. They may be "medical" in terms of keeping a
surgeon's sneeze out of an open surgery, but at minimum,
N95 to N100 (non-vented) is the only responsible route to
protecting your health.

The most troubling aspect of all this is the monetization angle.
Why were pharmaceutical companies passed sequencing of
CV in November of 2019? How exactly did Dr. Fauci see gain
of function research (increasing communicability of a virus) as
a good thing? The notion of communicable vaccines sounds
high-minded and proper. It also sounds like a bioweapon.
All comes down to payload.

Bugs, Nootropics, and *Nature*

There are two magazines you need to track if your plan is to
beat back Death a bit. One is *Life Extension* which has a dandy
publication covering the latest developments in vitamin
supplementation. The other is *Nature* which – accidentally or
on purpose – has been a great source for two of the best stories
in recent years about life extension.

The most recent one was *Nature*'s coverage of a *Study Finds* report. Tracking back from the lead in *Nature*, turns out in a Japanese research project, it was found that gut flora were the key to living a long life. Quoting Professor Kenya Honda, the *Study Finds* report cited this:

> "In particular, they have specific strains of an organism known as Odoribacteraceae. It makes bile acids that act as antimicrobials against a range of illnesses, the study finds. Experiments in mice showed they even destroyed hospital superbugs like Clostridioides difficile and Enterococcus faecium. They can cause severe diarrhea, especially in vulnerable people taking antibiotics.
>
> "These findings suggest specific bile acid metabolism may be involved in reducing the risk of infection – potentially contributing to the maintenance of intestinal health," Professor Honda says."

Which is right "next door" to eating healthy foods. Because yogurt, simple cheeses (Ricotta, Cottage) and kefir all have great gut biome enhancement potential. As was explained, every kind of disease and disorder can be impacted to some extent by fermented milk. Even systemic issues like high cholesterol.

Nature's biggest home run – in anti-aging – was a September 2019 report on a small study in California where people actually <u>ran their aging clock backwards.</u>

This study involved the use of human growth hormone (HGH), a diabetic drug (metformin) and DHEA which is a hormone precursor.

So far, I have not been able to talk my primary care physician into prescribing metformin for its off-label anti-aging aspects. But being lazy, changing PCPs or going wild on high fructose corn sugar to trigger diabetes doesn't sound easy, either. On the risk side, there have been recalls of time-release metformin, so extreme due diligence is wise.

Another one of those *"Hmm…what to do?"* moments you run into.

The Biology Basics

If you haven't read deeply into the aging process, terms like Telomeres may not be clear. Simply, and this won't be precise (but then this is not medical advice, either):

> "Telomeres are specialized nucleoprotein structures located at the ends of linear chromosomes; they consist of TTAGGG repetitive sequences. They function to prevent natural chromosomal termini from activating the DNA damage response."

The problem is telomeres are *not* indestructible. They have a useful life. Cycle limits.

What shortens them (literally), and their useful life are free radicals in the body. These are "oxidants" and – since oxidizers speed up reactions like rust and Jeff Bezos' sky toys – they *burn off the ends of telomeres*. This happens every time cells go through the birth and death process down at the microscopic level. Telomeres are beset with something called the "end replication problem."

Easiest thought of as? Burn enough off, live long enough, and go through enough cycles, and the telomere loses its protective functions. It suffers and on the job failure and apoptosis (cell death) comes along. Aging speeds up. Add sugars and more free radical sources if you're "already packed and in a hurry."

In fact, that's not a bad way of thinking about aging: Rusting from the inside out. With the *WD-40* of life being things like the metformin, HGH, DHEA mix and antioxidants. Or our own spin on this, which is far cheaper. Stick around.

The telomeres can be preserved and/or lengthened through both the "cocktail" approach (*Nature*, 2019) or, more recently, the rising interest in a supplementation process attempting to stimulate "direct methylation" by taking a supplement stack that seems to "like" the ragged end of telomeres.

The problem with all this telomere stuff is that it's long lead-time therapy. Another great catch by *Nature* was a 2015 article from the European Journal of Clinical Nutrition (damn, must have forgotten to renew that one!) that explained (pay attention here):

> "Our findings suggest that diet in the remote past, that is, 10 years earlier, may affect the degree of biological aging in middle-aged and older adults."

Which – for a lot of us – has to be terribly disappointing, though it makes sense. It would be great if a "deathbed realization" and change of diet could save us all. But the lag times are awful. Mainly because the body turns over some cells as infrequently as 7 or 8 years…

Bottom line? You needed to find that *Ponce de Leon* fellow's water bottle a long time ago to really beat the clock.

Hydration

I go back and forth on this one.   Medical types tell us that to keep the body working at top efficiency we should drink this *huge* amount of water every day.

Let me show you the numbers (snagged from the *Mayo Clinic* site): "About 15.5 cups (3.7 liters) of fluids a day for men. About 11.5 cups (2.7 liters) of fluids a day for women." Converts to 125 fluid ounces for men and 91 ounces for women. We assume this to be body weight dependent.

So, for example, if I weighed (glances around and drops into a whisper) 220 pounds and if the study average used was 175-pound males, then I really ought to bump up the water by 25.7 percent. But this means almost 160-ounces of water a day! 8-ounces isn't much, as any confirmed beer guzzler will tell you, but 160 ounces would be 14 ½ beers worth. I don't care who you are, that means a lot of poddy breaks! (*Mayo* didn't mention how much of the fluid could be beer…)

All-in, 6 ounces for a morning vitamin stack and 24 ounces of coffee plus one or two 8-ounce glasses and that can get me to martini time. In the interest of health, I do consume 30 ounces of water with suitable "adult flavorings." But no way anywhere near 160 ounces. Little over half?

Periodically, I will go on a "structured water binge" and guzzle 16 ounces times five. But that leaves me peeing every hour, or so and that gets in the way of work.

See how this works? On the other hand, maybe the gout
would be better, the sodium levels lower, resulting in lower
blood pressure. But adding 10 minutes a day of pee trotting
just…well…*you know…*

Food and Supplements

As an aging person, if you want to see your Personal Care
Physician flip-out on you, consider a discussion about adding
supplements. The answers you get may be all over the place
because a lot of doctors look at supplements as quackery. This
type of PCP may tell you about quality issues (supplements
are largely made overseas, but so are our cell phones and
cars…). They may claim organic food should be plenty. In
which case they have likely not read deeply on soil depletion.

You might ask your PCP to Google something simple (like
"soil depletion and declining nutrition") and see how they do.

Scientific American is a good source; see their article "Dirt Poor:
Have Fruits and Vegetables Become Less Nutritious? Because
of soil depletion, crops grown decades ago were much richer
in vitamins and minerals than the varieties most of us get
today."

This was an April 27, 2011, report. 10-years go! All you need
to do is wonder "Is it possible that 7-billion people eating
foods from the thin layer of remaining soil *possibly* are still
depleting soil like mad? And if "Yes", then should I take
supplements as cheap insurance?" Duh.

I've had extensive eye surgeries. I think the left eye is up to 5 (or 6 if you count touch-up for a leaking wound closure). When my young and very skookum specialist gifted cornea Doc said, *"Be sure to take an AREDs formula vitamin,"* my faith in supplements was sealed.

So, what is AREDS and why put faith in it? Two *Wiki* clips. AREDS (1) first:

> "The Age-Related Eye Disease Study (AREDS) was a clinical trial sponsored by the National Eye Institute, one of the National Institutes of Health in the United States. The study was designed to
>
> - investigate the natural history and risk factors of age-related macular degeneration (AMD) and cataracts, and
> - evaluate the effects of high doses of antioxidants and zinc on the progression of the two conditions in those with AMD."

This was followed (*in 2006) by the AREDS2 study. Again, a *Wiki* pull quote:

"The [AREDS2) study was a five-year look designed to test whether the original AREDS formulation would be improved by adding omega-3 fatty acids; adding lutein and zeaxanthin; removing beta-carotene; or reducing zinc In AREDS2, participants took one of four AREDS formulations: the original AREDS formulation, AREDS formulation with no beta-carotene, AREDS with low zinc, AREDS with no beta-carotene and low zinc. In addition, they took one of four additional supplement or combinations including lutein and zeaxanthin (10 mg and 2 mg), omega-3 fatty acids (1,000 mg), lutein/zeaxanthin and omega-3 fatty acids, or placebo.

The study reported that there was no overall additional benefit from adding omega-3 fatty acids or lutein and zeaxanthin to the formulation. However, the study did find benefits in two subgroups of participants: those not given beta-carotene, and those who had very little lutein and zeaxanthin in their diets. Removing beta-carotene did not curb the formulation's protective effect against developing advanced AMD, which is important given that high doses of beta-carotene have been linked to higher risk of lung cancers in smokers. According to Dr. Emily Chew, "Because carotenoids can compete with each other for absorption in the body, beta-carotene may have masked the effect of the lutein and zeaxanthin in the overall analysis."

As of now, I take an AREDS2 formulation which includes vitamins C, E, minerals zinc and copper, plus lutein and zeaxanthin.

Your Personal Chemistry Lab

It's my personal opinion that taking a solid multi-vitamin is the cheapest insurance you can buy. As we age, the chemistry of the gut changes, absorption rates decline, and the food today is not as nutritious as it was back in the 1960s. Nor is it full of genetic modifications.

Realizing this, Elaine and I took it upon ourselves to invest a small fortune in supplements over the past 10-years. We didn't have a lot (in fact very little) blood work done. But we each make careful note of what "made us feel better" and which things didn't help us feel more "amped."

One "get started" was to have our DNA workups done by 23andme.com. This told us a great deal about our "chemical selves" including dialing in where our highest risks are. CVD for me and thrombosis (her) and we both have one "Alzheimer's probability gene."

In addition, despite family word of mouth, the testing gave us a much clearer idea of what part of the physical world our bodies were optimized for. As a result, we tend toward foods native to that region. All very obvious when someone says it, but all invisible in modern medicine because that's such a damned "reactive" business that bouts of proactive research can be eyed (especially with a senior) as being "touched" or "eccentric." Perhaps. But we've paid for the ticket and it's our ride.

Again – **THIS IS NOT ADVICE** – but these are things we noticed:

- Elaine seems to thrive on a bit of additional vitamin B12, B6, biotin, magnesium, C60 (yes, carbon fullerenes in Olive oil), lithium orotate, and a multivitamin.
- In addition, we both have a morning and evening "stack" designed to roll back some aging chemistry.
- I need to avoid too much wheat, adding magnesium, C60, lithium orotate, and a saw palmetto and Swedish flower pollen (for "men's health") and a huperzine-A. In addition to a BP med which will disappear if I drop 30 pounds. (Mentally, this is my "pastry and seconds" pill. We're like the "reciprocal couple" to "*Jack Spratt could eat no fat...*" Medium rare and a good char on it, please. Few shakes of *Johnny's Dock* or *Weber's* on it, too...)

Since we both carry one of two "Alzheimer's genes" C60, lithium, and huperzine (me) - or whatever her experiment *du jour* happens to be - are high priorities not found in a daily vitamin.

We also take a daily baby aspirin because in the event we get a serious dose of "the *Rona*" there are indications that low dose aspirin can prevent the "stickiness of platelets than may lead to micro clotting. One study I read suggested a 27% reduction in death risk which beat *no* reduction, obviously!

Plan for Illness, Get Good Insurance

All the focus on intrinsic health pays off when bad juju shows up.

OK, we might sound daft (or, at least pill-happy) to a skeptic, we really feel great. We spent a lot of time researching insurance. A key lesson in how death sneaks up on us.

Elaine had two total hip replacements this year (2021).   The first in early February involved a small fracture (necessitating banding) of her femur. Recovering from that was a little slower than we'd hoped. But that was also (the week following surgery) when the East Texas Blizzard of '21 rolled through. Dumped more than 9-inches of snow and got down to 6-degrees F with rotating power outages.

She was able to snuggle in a nice warm bed because as part of being seriously "off-grid/break-down ready, we have a propane heater and a full 500-gallon tank (which is about 400 gallons useable.

Second surgery? May 18 and her *"Get out of here and come see us for an annual check in June of 22"* came in just 8-weeks.

Why did it go so well? Simple: She's in great shape! And this is when all that time working out, and supplements, comes back, and pays dividends. Recovery was simply remarkable.

By the way, if you ever have a hip or leg fracture, something we learned (from an emergency ambulance ride and ER visit) is that there is a "pain window" about 3-weeks after a major (bone involved) surgery like the banded right femur. Didn't happen with the unbanded left leg, though.

What seems to happen is there's a point where the nerves and brain are re-establishing their repartee. As they do so, the messaging (experienced as PAIN) can be 48-hours of terribly intense anguish. Answer? More pain meds. As a buddy who's a pain doc, later told me (usefully, *before* the second surgery) *"Give her more [meds] until she just begins to "snow out" a bit…then try to get her to go to sleep."*

That little lesson was $3,500 in ER bills, out of which all but about $600, or so, was covered by our Medicare *Advantage* plan. We figure our total out of pocket costs will be about $3,000 to $4,000 for the year. Maybe less.

As a general rule (applied to teeth, too): As soon as something pops up on your healthcare radar over age 50, or so, jump on it right away. When young, you can push around *Fate* a bit. Over 50, *Fate* pushes back. You need to stay on top of your health because *"the seat of your soul"* needs to be kept in good working order.

Morning and Evening Vitamin Stacks

Should mention – while still in advanced Age-Beating – that we take two critical "stacks" of pills morning and night. These are loosely based on anti-aging studies we have read.

The morning stack consists of Vitamins D, Vitamin A, folate, betaine, and resveratrol. Combined, this is a powerful slug of antioxidants. Just wish I could remember where I read the study on it.

The nightly stack is easy. It's loosely a home-cobbled
equivalent using OTC pills to approximate that 2019 study in
Nature I was telling you about. With a few tweaks.

The tweaks and pills are:

- DHEA is widely available. A quality pill with good
  customer reviews on *Amazon* or *Vita Cost* is fine.
- Since my PCP and I are doing the "slow dance" on
  metformin, a lot of the same blood sugar moderation
  effects can be achieved taking *berberines*. Again, a
  reliable brand.
- And, in place of Human Growth Hormone (God-
  awful expensive) there's the over-the-counter
  precursors: 5-HTP being the main one. Secondary,
  and while dozing off, 10-20 mg of *melatonin* is
  dissolved under the tongue. The "sublingual"
  tablets are designed for this use.

The main evening stack goes in an hour or two before
bedtime. The *melatonin* is the sendoff.

This timing was selected because HGH peaks naturally in
most people in the early hours of sleep when most repair
work is being done by the body. Comes in pulses, which is
why 8-hours is a good target for sleep. But the biggest comes
before midnight and that's when you want to have the 5-HTP
and melatonin in to assist that HGH peak in getting up into
optimum levels.

Using Brain Levers Less

Especially if you use lithium orotate (and have done your research because you can over-do this stuff, talk to a healthcare professional and track with blood work!) you may find the traditional "starters" and "ending" *social medications* may fade from your life.

Personally, I used to be comfortable having a nice (romantic) dinner and 3 to 6 shots of vodka (as well watered "talls"). But, down to a single shot or *maybe* two glasses of wine lately.

I think some of this is also from learning to face Death squarely. Now, when the question pops up (as it will with *everyone* from time to time) "What's the worst that could happen?" The answer is a lot clearer.

It IS going to happen, so let's be ready – better than 99% of people – and do this thing as "right" as possible.

Then, on waking the next morning, the need to jump into manic modern life is just a bit relieved, so a little less jack-up-juice is needed.

A Well-Scheduled Life

Afternoon martini is usually sipped in the "180-Room." So named for 180-degree views around the property. On my cocktail table is a yellow pad and on it, I have a "rough map" of the week's schedule.

The major events of the week are listed. Not just work, though. Even the "fun" and "spontaneous" things are blocked in. As I'm fond of telling Elaine: "Sure let me schedule some spontaneous time for us…"

She scowls then smiles. Because while scheduling spontaneity makes no sense to her, I'm really diligent about doing what I say.

This seems to be important for me (ADHD people may need it more than *normies* like her).

It reminds me that life is always about balancing. Lots of work, time for love, and time for art and creativity.

A lot of times, people get so wrapped up in what they're doing at the moment that they obsess. Which is hard on balance.

One other thing about schedules. Run (don't walk) to Amazon and get a copy of Cal Newport's book *Deep Work*.

Newport makes a very convincing case that if you don't block out *serious time* (like 5-hour and longer blocks) to get Big Important Work done, you can get mired down in minutia.

Personal interpretations are welcome. But I have two piles of "work" in my head. One's the "functional stuff." Get the mail, pay the bills, make a food run, mow yard, fix faucet, weed-eat, change bug traps and spray, water garden, weed…clean BBQ, get propane, pick up gas for mower. That kind of stuff.

These don't require much (if any) *brain work* because it's all well-worn process. It's the doing, not the thinking.

The Deep Work pile (with a nod to Newport) are the big blocks of time to:

- Write a book
- Print on the 3D printers or CNC machine, like a circuit board
- Make something in the wood shop
- Do something fun in the studio
- Time machine experiments
- Invent radical new ham radio antennas
- Participate in a ham radio contest (Morse code)
- Add a big-ass LED light bar to the Kubota for night work
- Weld up a new BBQ design…

When you have two piles like this (routine and Deep work [more fun]), you will find yourself springing out of bed in the morning. The deep work is the fun. Best saved for after the minutia is out of the way.

I sometimes can't wait to get started on the (messy, boring) *functional crap* I have pulled out of the hat for the day. Because as soon as that's all done, I can do what I love which is something from the Deep Work pile. (Today's life lottery drawing pulled the *Work on Book* ticket out…)

If you find you have less energy and Life isn't as exciting as you age, ask yourself if you have a lack of fun Deep Work you want to get done before "Check-out Time?"

When you grab hold of those projects, suddenly, living to 150 would not be enough.

You need Big Important Work so there's a reason to "hang around Life."

This ends our discussion of "hedging getting in the Box" that goes six feet under.

Next, we'll whip out Microsoft Project (though I'll use *Libre Project* which is free) and get to work on organizing the Big Important Work yet to be accomplished.

17. Basic Death "Optimizations"

"How the hell do you "Optimize" death and dying?"

Um… yeah. Let's blue sky that for a moment.

You wake up one morning and you're *dead.* (OK, skipping the wake-up part…)

- Surviving Spouse needs to be taken care of.
- Heirs may be circling like little sharks.
- Government wants its due.
- Scammers and liars will catch the scent of "easy money."
- Your legacy is important. Your heirs won't think to ask about it in advance.

A lot of this will be covered when we get into the Project Design chapter. Dying is a *project,* after all.

First thing, though? One of the problems with dying is *there are no do-overs.* When you're gone, that's the end. *Finis.* No coming back to re-live the final six years of life.

Credits roll, maybe on the way out; with luck after the Life Review Experience. But there is simply no way to "come back" (that we know of) to set things "right." Doesn't mean the scamming of seances won't be tried. You need to do what I call "Gullibility and Phishing Training" too.

Plan "Sunset Finances" Early On

A lot of young people (even our own offspring) look at the old people and might mentally go through the Heir Calculations:

- The old people are worth x.
- Their cost of dying shouldn't exceed y.
- The "heir pool" might be (x - y) = z
- The number of heirs is n.
- My "take" could be z / n.
- No income tax up to a few million, so yah-hah!
- Partee!

But here's the reality of it: When (or IF) a senior (who has not gamed things out in advance) goes into a long-term care facility, it oftentimes leads to immediate *liquidation of all assets*. There goes the ancestral homestead. A few dollars are allowed for "personal necessities", but this can be as little as $60 a month.

"No problem…if mom (or dad) goes into a home, we'll sell off the house and make sure they're taken care of…."

Not so fast, Bucko!

That doesn't work. The reason it doesn't is that old people often go into nursing facilities where their care (in the end) is largely funded by <u>Medicaid</u>. Rules vary from State to State.

Here in Texas, for example, in order not to have property counted as an asset, the Medicaid "Look-Back" window is (presently) *five-years.*

Say Elaine and I both have strokes the same day and need to be tossed in a home. The heirs might look forward to splitting up our meager assets. BUT under Medicaid rules, unless the sale of our primary residence happened (at a reasonable price and with solid documentation) 5-years ago, or longer, the money from that sale would be calculated as owing to Medicaid as a portion of payments.

This is dressed up in "screw little people clothing" and labeled as the Medicaid Lookback Rules.

Sound crooked? Well, yes – but no. You see, it's not right to totally stick it to the government for your last few years of reruns on the couch. But, to go back five years/60-months seems a bit hard, too.

The way to get around this is to sell the property (at an agreed upon price well in advance) and make sure that the sales price is somewhere approaching reasonable.

Another issue that pops up with certain kinds of property? Making sure that the property doesn't change *tax category,* as well if you have used special tax rules. Our little slice of Texas is as Ag land (tree farm), and we really do raise and sell timber.

Thing is, if we sell the property to heirs, what happens to the Ag exemption benefit? It would need to be redone. And other special tax benefits of being a senior go *"Poof!"* One of these is freezing of property taxes from 65-on. In our case, that will up the monthly nut by about $100. In some cities, that can press you into the $800+ rent (to government as property taxes).

Spreadsheet Time

What follows is a simple financial modeling exercise.

If Elaine and I were looking to ensure a decent Pay-Day for the surviving spouse and heirs, our best option might be to sell the ranch to one of the heirs who's trustworthy. We could also execute a long-term rental agreement for some pre-agreed figure which would lock in our low rent for, oh, 20-years, or so.

Thing is when the property changes hands, into the trust, the homestead exclusion could change. Frozen property taxes unfreezing can be painful because it might mean property taxes will go way up!

Another option would be to put the property in an irrevocable trust (meaning the grantors (the oldsters) couldn't have anything to do with the Trust Property operations, dispersal, decisions, or whatever. And CRITICALLY it would have to be in place at least five-years before the Medicaid issues comes up because of the Look-Back rules. With one state (California) offering a shorter lookback.

People put a lot of emphasis on planning for retirement when comes to money. But the bulk of most people's "going away" present to the heirs is in stocks, real estate, and other assets that need to be protected by a trust.

The most interesting late life parenting judgment then becomes: Which one of my children is the most trustworthy to run a family trust?   Go visit the website MedicaidPlanningAssistance.org. All but one state uses 60-months. California uses 30-months. Which is generous, but a closer comparison of facilities and standards of care should be undertaken before making decisions. In general, care for the money can be higher in lower wage states and away from urban areas.

Tradeoff here is how far do you expect anyone to drive to come see you? I can't count the number of 100-mile round trips from north of Seattle to Tacoma, Washington when my dad was sunsetting. It did influence when a "drop it" could just happen. When you're working, 2 ½ hours of travel and a like number of visiting hours adds up to a 5-hour block.

When you're at peak of your working life and trying to balance children into the mix, that's a big bite.

With Covid, the odds of drop-in's has fallen off, we'd expect.

Basic Health Data and Labs

Here's another one the heirs might not be "ahead of the curve on" – but rest assured, they *will all die, too.*

When their time comes along, they will genuinely appreciate your foresight if you leave them two cornerstones of future medical care improvement which no one talks about. Death is too scary, and people freeze up? Maybe…

The first is a concept I call "medical logging."

Of course, like many things we talk about in our *Peoplenomics.com* reports, this one isn't really "out there" yet. But the *need* is obvious. So, the intersectional void will be filled. Just a matter of *when*.

Let me show you what a medical log entry might look like for your (blood) heirs:

DATE: April 7, 2021
Event: Bi-Annual Healthcare Check

Basic Lab results:

Metric	*Mine*	*Range*	*Flag*
Glucose	96 mg/dL	70 - 110 mg/dL	
BUN	22 mg/dL	9 - 20 mg/dL	H
Creatinine, Ser	1.20 mg/dL	0.50 - 1.40 mg/dL	
GFR MDRD	60 mL/min	>=60 mL/min	
Sodium	140 mmol/L	137 - 145 mmol/	L
Potassium	4.8 mmol/L	3.5 - 5.3 mmol/L	
CO2 - Bicarbonate	32.0 mmol/L	22 - 30 mmol/L	H
Chloride	102 mmol/L	100 - 108 mmol/	L
Anion Gap	6 mmol/L	8 - 16 mmol/L	L
BUN/Creatinine Ratio	18	12 - 20	
Osmolality Calc	282	275.0 - 295.0	
Calcium	10.1 mg/dL	8.4 - 10.2 mg/dL	
Protein, Total	7.3 gm/dL	6.3 - 8.2 gm/dL	
Albumin	4.6 gm/dL	3.9 - 5.0 gm/dL	
Albumin/Globulin Ratio	1.7	1.1 - 2.0	
AST	40 IU/L	7 - 59 IU/L	

ALT   55 IU/L   0 - 50 IU/L   H
Alkaline Phosph.   51 IU/L   38 - 126 IU/L

I will also include in my "medical pack" other (more
confidential type information) like my (high) cholesterol
readings.

As involved as my son is in medicine (firefighter/EMT/Covid
team leader) it might be useful to know some of my "other
numbers" too as he gets on down the road:

Component	Your Value	Standard Range	Flag
Glycohemoglobin (GHb),Total %	5.5 %	4.8 - 5.9	
Estimated Average Glucose	111 mg/dL	mg/dL	

Now, the use of this for any of my offspring, would be to say
"Here's what my dad was doing at age 72…

About here, you should be slapping yourself on the head.
"OMG it would have been so useful to know how this metric
(or that) in these medical tests was known for when mom and
dad were my age. It might give me some insight into personal
healthcare…"

That's just the start…it gets even more obvious.

The DNA Based Medical Revolution

Virtually *no one I know* has both **a)** run their DNA sequencing and **b)** shared what those implications are with their heirs and offspring. How the hell do you miss *that one?*

Both Elaine and I had our DNA run several years ago. And she emailed the report to her closest son, so he'd have a copy. I emailed my results to my (medically inclined) son, as well.

If you haven't done the 23andme.com (or any of the others available like Ancestry.com) and then run it through services like *Self-Decode* you are missing tremendous insights into your healthcare future. Stuff even your doctor doesn't know right now!

Seriously, I have gotten as much from my DNA results as from my twice annual healthcare visits, in some regards. No, they won't prescribe anything. What they *will* do is tune-up your "spider senses" to be on the lookout for certain things.

Like what?

Well, here are some of my major risks:

Gene: gs141
2x risk of Alzheimer's disease You carry one APOE-ε3 allele and one APOE-ε4 allele. This results in 2x-3x increased relative risk of Alzheimer's disease compared to those carrying two APOE-ε3 alleles. For non-Caucasians the risk is increased, but SNPedia has not yet seen any reliable estimates. This is based on
- rs429358(C;T)
- rs7412(C;C)

Another risk?

Sequence: rs1333049(C;G)
1.5x increased risk for CAD 1.5x higher risk for coronary
artery disease
rs1333049 has been reported in a large study to be associated
with heart disease, in particular, coronary artery disease. The
risk allele (oriented to the dbSNP entry) is most likely (C); the
odds ratio associated with heterozygotes is 1.47 (CI 1.27-1.70),
and for homozygotes, 1.9 (CI 1.61-2.24). This SNP has also
been reported to have the highest association of any SNP
studied in a subsequent experiment conducted with the
resources of the German MI [Myocardial Infarction] Family
Study.

To me, this was fascinating stuff to learn *before the onset of any
illness.* Because it allowed me to begin a proactive life-style
change that has included a lot more exercise and very diligent
use of huperzine-A, melatonin, and increased lithium uptake
because there is *some* suggestion that lithium deficiencies may
express as dementias and possibly Alzheimer's in the
literature. (Not medical advice).

Also, a Spousal Benefit

First half of 2021, Elaine had two total hip replacements done.
Thanks to having her DNA on hand, I was able to email her
doctor just prior to the first surgery:

"Feb 3, 9:30 AM
Ref DNA data run of Elaine Petersen (Ure) right hip surgery
sked 2/8/21.

Forgot to mention in PAS two DNA sequencing notes on
Elaine: (23andMe sequencing, Promethease report)

rs6025(A;G)   3.5-4.4x risk of thrombosis (ref url
https://www.snpedia.com/index.php/rs6025)

gs153 CYP2C19 Extensive or Ultra-Fast Metabolizer
CYP2C19 Ultra-rapid Drug Metabolism. Medicines
metabolized by CYP2C19 (ref url:
https://www.snpedia.com/index.php/gs153)"

Now, I don't know if that was useful to her doctor, or not.

But I can assure you if I was a doctor and I knew that someone
on *my* table had an elevated thrombosis risk and was a fast
drug metabolizer, that *might* have been useful very short-term
information to have going into the OR. Just in case.

Over time, I think, a lot more of this (DNA-AS – my acronym
for *DNA Augmented Surgery*) will become a lot more common.
Since medicine is – at some level – the long-term expression of
our DNA. Plus, environmental "adders" and minus
environmental "detractors."

It may be many years into the future, yet. Still, when we look
ahead to how we might "die better" any old time, now?

Some "data care packs" which could be of use for better
informing our offspring and heirs medically in the future, sure
seems like it could be at least as valuable as some silly paper-
denominated financial asset.

Knowing as you do now (hopefully) from reading this book
that we are spiritual knowledge beings who have just put on a
body for a while – like you might a favorite jacket – the gifts
and leave-behinds that will have the most <u>utility value</u> will be
informational in nature.

Sharing our learning and loving over a lifetime is a marvelous investment to make.

Put yourself in the shoes of anyone you deeply care about and ask *right now*: What is the knowledge or information that they might find useful when I'm gone? That's how you really begin packing to die.

18. Organizing for "Successful Death"

The last step of dying seems pretty easy: You just don't wake up. Or, if already awake, you just go "back to sleep" and *then* you don't wake up.

We need a process, though, so we don't miss details. I propose:

- Organizing personal documents and papers
- Death's To-Do list
- Tasking, and Directives
- Test Dying
- Revisions and implementation

Before getting to that final step, implementation, there's a lot of "stuff" to go through. Just tons of it.

Wrote it all down in a *Peoplenomics* subscriber newsletter some time back, which (magnanimously) I've authorized myself to include parts of here.

"Is Your Life "Organized-Enough" to Die?"

Mine didn't used to be - true fact.

I had one of those moments of brutal honesty about taxes maybe 9-years ago. I was feeling anxious and was talking to our tax attorney (my *consigliere*) about my uneasiness should I ever be audited by IRS. Got all the paper but box after box…all honestly done, but a stress source anyway.

"What you need to do is get a scanner. You need to keep it on and next to your desk so that everything you are billed for – or money received – is documented…Get a good one. It's a legit business expense."

Two things have put my mind at rest about audits ever since: I never cheat on taxes – and in fact more often than not err on the side of generous with the government. I never wrote off a dime of my airplane, for example. Second aspect of being IRS Audit-Proof is having the by God backup paper. Swear, I could document a fart if I had to.

The same concept applies when getting ready to Die.

A few years back I decided that when I depart Earth, I'd like to do so in a <u>highly organized</u> fashion. However, I also wanted to spend a minimum of my remaining time doing paperwork. Life is for enjoying, after all! I also wanted to make sure Elaine would have a "plug and play" set of modest monthly bills and other than food and medical co-pays would be able to live a relaxed life.

No hassles and an annual bill checklist. Dream stuff. Who has that operating plan in place for their spouse, though?

In 2012 I did a Peoplenomics report on the high-speed scanner. That article (A 2013 Resolution: Finally Going Paperless, *Peoplenomics #591-B*, December 22, 2012) outlined my purchase of a high-end scanner and getting it implemented. It makes my life *flow*…

"To be sure, moving to a 100% "scanned life" hasn't been the be-all, end-all answer to paper. After scanning, every bill is stamped "SCANNED" and still goes into the annual IRS documentation drawer. But having <u>everything</u> scanned (and sorted into folders) allows me to do our taxes each year <u>in a single day</u> (in early February) and get the refund back in mid-March.

Well, except Tax Year 2020s March 31, 2021, filing which was submitted on the last day of the month. Result? We didn't get the TY2020 refund until mid-July 2021. <u>Never file on the last day of the month</u>, is the takeaway!

At the highest level, the software that came with my scanner, a Fujitsu *ScanSnap* iX500 Scanner for PC and Mac (PA03656-B005) with Adobe *Acrobat Pro* (it was $433 in 2013) allows me, just like any other business I've managed, to break things apart into staff and line functions.

An inflation note: As of August 2021, the equivalent Fujitsu ScanSnap iX1500 Deluxe Color Duplex Document Scanner with Adobe Acrobat Pro DC for Mac or PC, is still just $586 at *Amazon*. And it has 89% five-stars from users. I'd give mine 6-stars, if I could. But knock-off 1 star because the *SanSnap Organizer* doesn't zoom (yet). So, with some vision impairment, sorting to different folders means a lot of squinting. I really shouldn't bitch, though…

In a business, the "staff" includes the accounting and legal departments, and the "line" is the group of people that actually makes the product that people pay money for. Oftentimes, the bean counters and lawyers think they are the reason for a company's success, but I've never seen this to be the case.

99.99999% of the time, it's great product and great people. The small other percentage may be sports lawyers, but that's a thorn for another morning.

Just like in a business, I label my two "highest level" filing cabinets "Accounting" (which includes legal) and "Operations" like so:

When the + button is pressed, in either department, you get down into the folders where each of life's major interfaces is stored. My wife (and the key people likely to survive me) have access to almost ANY financial paperwork this way. Everything is in here:

- My ScanSnap
  - Accounting
    - Ad Revenue
    - Advertising Contracts
    - Bank Deposits
    - BirthCertMarriage
    - Deductions
    - EIN George
    - Farm Unit
    - Healthcare and medical notes
    - Insurance
    - Investments
    - IT
    - Legal
    - Licenses
    - Non-Competes - NDAs
    - Passwords & Reg
    - Publisher Contracts
    - Resume
    - Social Security
    - TAX ARCHIVES
    - Trademarks
    - TVEC
    - Utilities
    - Vendors
    - Warranty Returns
    - Wills

Additional [+] boxes open more levels. Under Tax Archives, there's Texas Sales Tax and the Federal returns. Along with County Property Taxes, too.

The VERY First Thing is a "Dead Letter"

Don't pick up and write anything yet. Let's do more "thinking out loud" here.

First, the Dead Letter project is set up for three "use cases." The first is YOU die. The second is YOUR SPOUSE dies. The third choice is you BOTH DIE.

Each of these will have a specific set of "ideal actions" associated with it.

I know I said don't write anything down yet – but it's OK to open Excel and label column 1 "Use Case." Column 2 "Action Step". We'll add details as we go.

This is a set of bullet points, more than anything, but other columns might be usernames and account passwords and such, to be tackled by your executor(s). Part of your deliverable may be in a Word doc and part in the *Excel* or *Project* file. Depending how complex your estate is, *Excel* is likely sufficient.

MS Project (or free *Libre Project)* gets useful if you have properties and illiquid assets to sell off.

Excel still supports links to get to account login pages. And you can copy from the password column into the browser. We don't need to go overboard on the software. Just remember for every 100 *Excel* users you know, there are only 3-8 competent *Project* jocks.

This is Death we're planning. Not a *Gold Partner* application.

Obviously, a "dead letter" (the doc/docx details part) will address what's to be done with each of the relationships in each folder. Your paperwork piles and scanner folders will determine how you want each aspect of Life handled. Which is why the Dead Letter doesn't get off into *"Be sure to give grandson Jimmy that quarter I promised him."* Jimmy isn't in your Will because it's only a *quarter*. Executors, surviving spouses, heirs…that's what the Dead Letter is for.

If there are still heartstring issues you feel don't fit, you could make a list of those and work on ironing those out before moving to the Great Beyond. While you can still do something about them.

But before that level, a "newbie" to the computer systems around here would need a map. The deliverables include:

- Scope of work and map of process
- Instructions to the Executor(s)
- The *Excel* workbook with tabs for each major section of the Dead Letter
- The Dead Letter Itself (which with the *Excel* is really the guts of the dying well project.
- The Will and probate instructions
- The Spousal workplan and money budget/spending plans

- Spousal requests and directions
- Guidance on medical billing and burial

So, the opening of the "dead letter" is the Instructions part and it explains in detail *"How to log in to George's Life..."* The first page of mine is a list of web sites and online accounts to be taken down. Usernames and passwords are critical information so burn the Dead Letter to password protected media.

When updated copies of my CDs go out, the password is given verbally on a phone call.

Each computer on our home networks (there are 3 of 'em) is secured with sign-in credentials. If you are the I.T. department in your family, make sure to include name and logon for Admins isn't overlooked!

If you don't do this, just getting into the directory structure so that a computer can be searched for an old tax document (or whatever) can become an ugly task.

One more I.T. aspect? If you do serious work at home, remember that certain IT functions (like websites) may be secured such that they can *only* be accessed from certain IP addresses.

Also - if needed - the names of databases (MySQL, WordPress, and website usernames and passwords for admins, for example) are also included.

Next is where are the backups stored? Ever write down how to access the past *n* months of backups which are stored on rotating 1 TB SSDs?

Now, maybe you didn't think your Dead Letter was going to be long, but it MAY be. Sure, a router can be reset and placed on "open" for a while, but logging in through a 16-mixed character logon to Windows 10 on a critical computer?

And then finding the hidden directories where more sensitive information might live? That may go beyond the capabilities of most people I know. Not that people are "dumb" because they can't un-hide hidden directories. Maybe they're just smart in different areas, is more like it. Looking for hidden directories might not occur to them. And, what's your Microsoft user account for each computer? Not the PIN but the long-by God login? Does your Executor(s) have a clue?

Where are the documents and how to I get them? That's the very first step in redrawing the roadmap to your digital life. It's got to be detailed enough for a civvie to follow.

Oh, and don't forget the information in your Grimoire. (*"What's a grimoire?"*) From Wikipedia:

> "A grimoire /grɪmˈwɑr/ is a textbook of magic. Such books typically include instructions on how to create magical objects like talismans and amulets, how to perform magical spells, charms and divination and also how to summon or invoke supernatural entities such as angels, spirits, and demons.[1] In many cases, the books themselves are also believed to be imbued with magical powers, though in many cultures, other sacred texts that are not grimoires, such as the Bible, have also been believed to have supernatural properties intrinsically; in this manner while all books on magic could be thought of as grimoires, not all magical books could."

The grimoire might include your medical (MyChart) login, your MySSA.gov log in and things like that. Notes on property parcel names and so forth. Will notes.

The Grimoire is kept separate from the wills, separate from the Social Security cards (which were NEVER going to be used for identification, right? What a crock *that* was, huh? Government still lies, look surprised…).

Besides impossible to remember router logons, the kind of hardcopy information includes all the "shiny new" docs for websites and complex electronic logons like our logon to the TreasuryDirect account. (I told you bonds and gold a long time ago…)

If your life is complicated, the Grimoire can be digital (Word, or something common like PDFs on CD) or it can be hard copy, or both. The hard copies of software registration keys and so forth are useful, too. Secret work project keys and passwords....

Maps of where the gold is, the silver stash, the antidote for poisonings, and your Tinder Account. (Kidding!)

If your "lone gold coin" is someplace other than obvious, then your dead letter recipients should each have a personal key (something known only to you and them) that will decrypt that location. Making up treasure maps is fun and can keep the job light-hearted. Someplace on our property is a buried bottle of rum, too. Can't be serious all the time, can we?

I assume you know if burying *real treasure,* you know to bury it, then backfill a half foot of dirt, then lay some scrap steel atop it? Otherwise, metal detecting might find the right stash. But if you plant scrap all over hell and gone…well, let's assume you read *Treasure Island* and know what a pulse-induction detector is…

Create the Check List from Checks

A good starting place for any "dead letter" is to go through a year's worth of checkbook entries and figure out how to "turn off" all future bills. If I leave first, there would be a plan and details for the Executor(s) and Elaine.

In this category, there's the water, sewer, cable/satellite, internet provider, property taxes, car tags, home insurance, car insurance, airplane insurance (boat, or RV or whatever), various balances outstanding, and so forth.

An annual budget with spending ideas may be included.

Work through sale of "toys" ahead of time for the Executor. How to sell a boat/RV. airplane and then what to do with insurance and.....you can fill this in as you work through the Dead Letter and Excel file.

These highly detailed notes would, ideally, be broken down into one-time, ongoing-monthly, and annual repetitive tasks you've had to put up with in life.

If you've got everything in your electronic filing system, all
you need to do is tell your dead letter recipients what the
work plan is, where to find account numbers, passwords, and
so forth. Then everything can be consolidated into the go-
forward plan within a day.

And that's it.

Since Elaine and I each have one of the (dreaded) Alzheimer's
precursor genes, we are paying more attention as we age to
putting "Important Minutia" into durable (non-computer)
fiber-based information storage and retrieval systems. (paper
and pen!).

One of the things we've enjoyed doing is living an
occasionally stylish life. Seems only right that stylish people
will put out a little "front-end effort" unburdening those who
remain when we depart.

It makes a fine going away present.

Morbid title aside , the Dead Letter is not a trivial
undertaking. Especially if you have accumulated assets of any
consequence. So, it deserves proper thought and a weekend
when you have time to kick things around with the spouse.

Of course, we still live with the belief "the letter" will never be
read, but if (OK, *when*, but I'm still in denial here) it *is*, you
want it to be complete leaving zero loose ends.

My opening line sets the tone of mine:

> "Since I seem to be dead, I need your help closing out a
> few leftovers from life I couldn't take care of in
> advance. I've thought all this through, but if something
> isn't clear, I am trusting you to do the right thing.

To take care of the loose ends, you're going to need to use my main computer. And to do that, you'll need the username and login... There are two "process maps" of what needs to be done, depending on whether I'm survived by Elaine or whether we've both checked-out at the same time.

Before we start, let's look at the process of closing down George's Life..."

 And then you're into it...

Turns out the Wills were the easy part. Tell the attorney who gets what and sign and Witness. Done.

The Dead Letter is way more complicated. So is the accompanying spreadsheet workbook. Ugly? Sure. Still, it needs to be done and a little forethought now will ensure whoever straightens things up after you will find the hidden bottle of rum and that little something buried in the woods for their trouble.

19. First-Hand: The High Cost of Dying

My formal training (a distance learning BA & MBA before it was a popular option – something that changed with Covid...) drives a good part of the thinking behind my writing.

Both the UrbanSurvival (free) and Peoplenomics ($40/year) websites are highly focused on subjects of a general financial nature. Our particular Point of View, though, is miles from Mainstream Media ruts.

You see, money is not an "end in and of itself" any more than our short time on Earth is an "End in and of itself." It what you *get out it* that matters. Everyone wants to make money up to the end, but how many people inspect their own lives and play back highlights?

We therefore champion some very old-school notions that 'cover the waterfront' in economics and Life in general. Old notions that include "Someone always gets stuck for the bill" even if that's neither humane nor sane.

Sanity, regrettably, does not permeate the *Earthly Plane.* Accounting, however, seems to.

I said at the beginning of this book that while *overall* Life is like Thurow's zero-sum Game, that doesn't mean that individuals can all have fun. There are people who more regularly than most *do* get screwed and have seriously sucky *lives*.

For (in my flavor of nutjob accounting) if some people make it through Life having fun and great times, shouldn't that imply an accounting contrary ledger? This hints there could be up to an equal number of people in pain and suffering when compared with blissful and joyous.

More unfortunate is that double-entry accounting systems demand balanced books. Remember duality is what Life is all about, right? Up/Down, debit/credits.

Fitting then that one of our readers shared an eye-opening account of the True Cost of Dying if you don't plan for it. Personally-identifiable information has been removed but the cost numbers are 'factual actuals' from spring 2021:

> "I wanted to share with you my most recent experiences in the world of finances.
>
> 95 yo mother lived independently in her own condo- did her own cooking, cleaning, laundry, grocery shopping. April 3 this year, she tripped over an area rug and fell, breaking her femur just below her hip replacement (done in 2002).
>
> Easter emergency 4-hour surgery followed; recovering fine, went to rehab, where she improved daily (actually toe touch walked 80ft on the double bars).

--Hospital wanted to discharge her to the nursing/rehab facility Monday, April 5th ! I disagreed and had a knips fit and used the 'power words' - 'unsafe discharge', 'lack of continuity of medically provided services' "vital sign instability' 'initiating a Medicare Fast Appeal'.

I have to interject here because it is *critically important.* POWER WORDS. These include "Chief of Staff, 'unsafe discharge', 'lack of continuity of medically provided services' – all of which have the "ring of lawyers." Mysteriously, or not, healthcare is better when providers know you understand how to "play the game." That means speaking lawyerese.

Back to the reader's account:

> "--As a result, she (mom) remained in the hospital until April 9th (surprise!) at which time she was transferred to our pre-selected nursing/rehab facility. (She had rehabbed there in 2016 after a back surgery --back then the facility was one that I toured/reviewed (among many) so that we knew EXACTLY where she was going on the day of discharge).

> -Side note: Events gobble time: I was at the hospital every day with her from 6:30am - 5pm and was able to be an advocate not only for what she needed but also what was/wasn't being done. Yes, a VERY squeaky wheel but the loud one gets results. Every patient HAS to have an advocate that will fight for them and stand up for them. And be present to truly know what is going on.

--While at rehab, she was steadily improving every day. Once again, I was there every day - from 6:30am - 3 or 4pm. Making SURE that what was supposed to be/happen, did.

About 8 days in, I noticed that the surgical wound was still draining - not a lot but still. I kept bringing this up to the nurses, but they kept telling me it was o.k. I am no medical person, and because of the nature of the surgical area and the age, I thought they knew better.

--Day 14, they changed the wound dressing and within an hour, it had drained through bandage, nightgown, and top sheet. They decided to make an appointment with original surgeon for the next day.

We went the next morning, and she was given a round of serious oral antibiotics for the next 7 days because it was determined it was a staph infection.

By now she was starting to not do well.

--Day 21, meds ended.
--Day 23, infection returned with serious draining again and temp of 101.5
--She was then scheduled for a wound clean out surgery on May 5th, which went well, but it was found that the staph infection had gone into the bone.

-- Proposed aggressive treatment plan - run an IV line into arm with 6 weeks iv antibiotics and 2x week doc office visit (each time, of course, using a cabulance service that we pay for) followed by 3 months of oral antibiotics, followed by lifetime of antibiotics, which would have interfered with her other meds.

And of course, no guarantee of successful outcome. Mother was tired and said no and now totally bedridden - couldn't even sit up by herself. So only other option - hospice.

--Was given 3 days to find an appropriate facility for her.
--Worked with a 'reputable' local service to help narrow down options and places. Someone who has been doing this for years.

BTW – IMHO do NOT use 'A Place for Your M*m' - don't care about how they advertise it. It is a sca… Well, let's say an 'agent' contacts you and give you a list of places that they recommend. However, this agent could be sitting in NJ or California and has never ever stepped foot in or seen real time any of the recommended places.   And that *is* important because you want someone who has actually SEEN these places, Really KNOWS the owners/facilities, and knows who works where and came from where, etc.

So, for three days straight - every day, went to hospital 6:00am - 2pm, and then went to look at facilities 2:30-7pm(driving around here during rush hour still sucks).

We determined mother would need adult family home - they are limited to 6 patients, and a home type environment. Plus, they are quieter than a nursing home. And she needed full time 24/7care - eating, bathing, toilet, etc.

Some of the homes I saw - 1960s home where the bedrooms are the 'rooms' - where you have enough room for a twin-size bed, a nightstand, and a recliner - no room for a portable commode even - and 1 bathroom for 6 residents! Even in the hallways- enough room for 1 person to walk.

Another home I looked at was 'nice' - but the owners had been doing this for only 2 years. The proposed room was small, facing north, painted a darkish blue, and the window looked out onto the 'backyard', which, at the time, was littered with construction debris. Indoors, the 'residents' were placed in wheelchairs sitting in front of a communal tv.

So forth and so on. Some homes sat next to I-405; some overlooked the back of a grocery store, all except one (the one we selected) didn't have a/c. Most of the homes are run by a professional nurse however, the daily care is done by home 'aide' helpers - from what I saw - mostly from Kenya or Ethiopia or Mexico - usually 2 helpers per day/1 at night. And that night person doesn't have to be a 'wake' person - meaning they don't have to stay awake, just be able to get up if needed. (and of course, most of the places didn't have a way to 'call' for someone - some places suggested that the resident can call out; another said they would give her a bell she could ring....)

And these were the $7-9,000 month price range.

Even at the $11,000/mo. level - there were many things that were lacking.   But at least the surrounding environment was decent - newer building, view of a yard, quiet. Some homes the monthly 'rent' covers just about everything - others, you have to pay extra for things like food, adult diapers, shampoos/soap, etc. And if you need someone to take resident to doctors, they charge $50/an hour. So, again, ask a lot of questions. Write it all down.

But with adult family homes – be aware they all charge an 'administrative/admissions' fee - that is non-refundable.

Majority of the nicer ones have the month-to-month contracts - payable in advance, non-returnable for any reason (like our situation).

Then there was/is the Evergreen Hospital Hospice Care Center. (check out their website). Gorgeous place, highly skilled nursing staff 24/7, etc. - but like I said $20,000/mo. - and no, Medicare doesn't cover it...Medicare covers the cost of meds, but not the facility.

Back to the story: She had that second surgery May 5 to do a clean out of the infected area. Recovery didn't go well because they found the staph infection had gotten into the bone. Proposed course of action - aggressive treatments which, at 95, she just didn't want to do. She then agreed to go on hospice status. However, she was completely bedridden and the small home I have could not accommodate her needs.   I had to find a place for her where she could have 24-hour care.

Wanting a more 'homey' environment, I checked out many adult family homes here on the Eastside of Seattle (Bellevue, Issaquah, Woodinville, Kirkland).

A couple requirements were that it was within 30 minutes of my home, that she had a private room, there was a 'wake' night staff, and a monthly cost of $6-8,000/mo. Let me tell you - these places were depressing, and I didn't want her to spend her last days in such a place. So, I upped the monthly 'rent'. Found a place that fit the bill, she had a view of the garden, it was a newer home (6yo), had a/c (rare in PNW) AND a backup generator (even rarer) AND had an available bed. At $11,000/mo. Payable at the first of the month, PLUS a $3,000 administrative/admissions fee.

Fortunately, mother had long term insurance that covered $5,000/mo. - BUT it ONLY kicked in *after* we had paid out of pocket for 90 days, so we had to cover the rest.

Mother went into the adult family home May 14, with the Evergreen Hospital Hospice Team helping me and her. Weekly/bi-weekly nurse visits, chaplain visits, social services/worker visits - it was a GREAT relief to have them supporting us.

But mother couldn't get comfortable - because she couldn't do opioids, we were limited on how to keep her comfortable and pain free.

Things progressed from ok to worse, and finally, after trying many renditions and ways, the hospice nurse had my mother admitted to the Evergreen Hospice Care Center (across the street from Evergreen Hospital) on June 1st --- a LOVELY place- calm, peaceful, 24/7 full time very experienced hospice nurses. They were able to finally figure out the right combo of meds to keep her pain free, comfortable - basically catatonic but peaceful.

June 1st was also the day I handed over the June 'rent' check of $11,000 to the adult family home - thinking that once the meds were fine, mother would return there and this way her room was held until her return.

The Evergreen Hospice Center was everything that I was seeking and wanting for my mother's limited time. And they were more than willing to keep her there, BUT the monthly cost there is $20,000/mo.!!!

I was struggling to figure out how to make this work, how to afford this place for mother - given that they didn't quite know just how long she had - could be days, could be weeks, and if her body fights the infection, could be a month – or much longer. However, mother was tired, as was her body, and on June 6th, she passed away.

Now here is the catch: at most adult family homes around here contracts state that the monthly rent is for the *entire* month - whether she stays there or not. Didn't matter that she passed away - they get to keep the monies.

So, total cost for 18 days of care = $6,300 (month of May was pro-rated) plus $3,000 admin fee, plus $11,000 for June (and she didn't spend a single day there, but they 'held' the space) - equals $20,300.00 !!!!!!!!!!!!!!!!!!!!! And no long-term insurance kicked-in because we hadn't gotten to the 90 days out of pocket yet.

Moral of this experience (one that I NEVER would have imagined) -
either have family agree to take care of you at home (which is a 24/7 job - one that isn't always pleasant or easy.

OR: know that you will go broke and/or have to sell absolutely everything to provide and give the needed care.

Oh, and btw - if anyone has their home in a 'trust' - which was popular about a decade ago, which my mother did - know that you better have everything in order if you need to sell the place to get the money to afford these things, especially have a durable power of attorney naming who can make ALL your financial decisions for you and act upon those decisions.

Sorry for the length of this email cuz I know you don't like to read long ones - but dang, I wish I wish someone would have told me about this before it happened so we could have been better prepared - how -

- Have all legal dox updated and current
- Make sure that the durable power of attorney person is aware of just HOW much time, effort and work it will be. I was at the

> hospital every day - some days 8-12 hours and required to make all kinds of decisions.
> - Go visit assisted living/nursing homes/adult family homes ahead of time so you aren't pressured to make fast and quick decisions because of time constraints.
> - Make sure there are funds to cover initial expenses.

- Fortunately, I was a joint account holder on mother's checking/savings accounts so that I could write checks from her account to cover these costs...but she only had enough for 4 months - after that, if her home didn't sell, not sure what we would have had to do. And btw - she lived in her place 23 years - so not only did the place need to be given a good coat of makeup (paint, carpet, etc.) to sell, but getting rid of ALL that crap and stuff that was ONLY valuable to her, and no one else- took a lot of time and effort. So, start going through all that stuff now - please don't leave it for someone else.

This last action point is a personal "toughie" for me. After living an ultra-compressed life of everything dual-purposed, when possible, on a small sailboat for 10+ years, spreading out over 29 acres in the tall pines has been a joy.

This is all very grown-up and sad stuff.

As the summer progressed, the Reader's experience continued to unfold in not very pleasant ways:

> Well, here it is almost the end of July - this is how things have been progressing:

I insisted I wanted my husband as the Trustee of the Trust, over my attorney hesitations. My husband had to go and hire his own attorney to represent him. After several Zoom meetings, it was agreed upon that hubby could be Trustee, with, of course, his attorney. And I have no further say or control over things, even though all the proceeds go directly to me. (!)

Retainers provided, notices mailed, papers filed with courts... my mother's condo was finally listed for sale, offer was made/accepted, and things have moved along with documents being signed the 23rd and a closing of July 30th. All proceeds from sale go directly into the Trust, which trust has been set up by our investment banker, complete with EIN. With my husband, as Trustee, in charge of the Trust.

To reach this point has involved so much time and effort, and also expenses - thus far, between my attorney and hubby's atty - close to $10,000 in attorney expenses.

Here's another 'I didn't know' -

So, many of my mother's expenses, while alive, were paid from her checking account (all on auto-deduct/autopay), including things like secondary health insurance, homeowner's insurance, utilities, etc. Many of these were auto deducted the first few days of every month. She passed away on the 6th of the month, after these were paid. Thus, entitled to 'refunds'. BUT, because she has passed, these refunds are issued via paper checks, made payable to the 'estate of'...which, now, HAVE to be deposited into the Trust.

Finally, with the sale of her condo, I put in a request with the Post Office to forward mail (to receive all those things where I wasn't able to change the address - WHICH, btw, one NEEDS to have Power of Attorney to change - even after death. Fortunately, I had provided POA docs to all necessary entities (utilities, insurances, etc.) a couple years ago...so at least that wasn't as complicated for me, but there was one I had missed (her pension - that then required copies of her Will, the signed POA, death certificate....)

Anyhow…
…couldn't do the change of address online because the Post Office wants $1.05 to 'process' the change of address form online.

BUT - here is the catch, the credit card used to pay for this MUST have the original address on it - which my mother's didn't (for security reasons, the mailing address was changed to mine several years ago). So, couldn't do it online…

SO…
…went to my local Post office (Duvall, WA) and got a form. Filled it out. HANDED it to the postal employee behind the counter.

3 weeks later, still nothing being forwarded. Go online (Informed delivery) and find there is nothing on file for forwarding.

Initiate a 'where's my mail' inquiry with the p.o.   They said they didn't have anything on file and to go online and complete the form online...I tell them I can't and give reasons. They tell me to go to the post office where my mother's zip code is - the larger facility in Issaquah to complete another form...

SO...
...I go to the Issaquah post office. Stand in line. Get to counter. Ask for a change of address form.

Am told they don't have any forms - they are all out.

They tell me to go to another post office, that maybe they have some forms - there are 3 other post office locations I could try.   I get a little 'huffy'.   I ask to speak to the supervisor.

They reluctantly call for the supervisor over the PA system.   I wait. And I wait. And I wait - I am NOT leaving! 15 minutes later a supervisor appears. I explain situation. They say that yes, indeed, no forms - they can't seem to get any supply and when they do, they get just a few.

I insist... Supervisor feels sorry for me - goes into the back - comes back 5 minutes later with a form. I ask them to wait while I complete and hand back to supervisor.

NOW...
...6 weeks later, mail is just starting to show up. Although it is unknown where all the mail that DID show up during those 6 weeks, went.
So even something that USED to be so easy, no longer is.

Nothing is easy, nothing has been seamless. This End-of-Life crap is so difficult for the living.   Just shouldn't be that way.

That's one of the reasons I was driven to write this book. Because almost every aspect of Death in the modern world has such a *stigma* attached to it. Denial, postponements, rejections, cash requirements…seems to never end.

Above all – like buying or selling a home – everyone has their hand out and wants something.

20.   Dying's Not All Bad

Let's wind this up on something of a positive note. Some comments from another reader – this one who has worked years in healthcare. Much of his work life was in senior care facilities in the Midwest.

He tells some interesting stories about how it is people actually "pass over" at their end.

> "… having worked healthcare all of us working the floors have those stories. I have a couple that are my favorites. One came back because I messed up the bed making it, lol lol. It's my ultimate favorite though it scared the hell out of me. That patient lived three more years after a brief time dead.…
>
> The other one is the exercise bike. I worked in a really quiet area… there was an exercise bike that was put in storage until a family could travel back to sort through the belongings…
>
> About 1 am (more active during a thunderstorm) you could hear someone on that bike peddling like hell… lol lol.
>
> We would get new employees that would start and think there's no such thing (as ghosts). We would leave them at the office while we did patient rounds. We would come back, and they would always say "…you won't ever believe what happened…" LOL

My wife's favorite story is pancakes lol a patient *had to come back* for pancakes, lol..

Then there was this one guy who was real mentally abusive to his youngest daughter. He relentlessly blamed her for all his troubles. He died and was laying there. Just as staff were just going to zip-up the bag with the daughter bawling her eyes out, the guy sat upright and said, "Nothing was ever your fault Shawn…I was wrong, and God wants me to set it right." Whereupon he laid back down and was again quiet dead. They zipped the bag…"

And so, the familiar theme is showing again: At the micro level we all have choices. But at the macro level it's likely all a *zero-sum Game*. Like Gaussian noise distributions – choice all over the place spectrally. But in the end, the Noise like Life itself, is its own Entity.

Given what you know, it's clear which side of Accounts to stay on, right?

21.   A Hidden Law: Getting Over It

There's a war going on at our tree farm in the woods of East Texas. War on possums.

You see, just has a "vengeful God" smote some wrong-doers in ancient times, attacking the Israelites, so too when possums killed our feral white-face female cat, Elaine was devastated.

I take no joy in killing animals, especially possums. But emotionally, no problem because they have stolen (a cat and my wife's happiness) from us.

What I seem to be walking in are "footprints of the Gods" to borrow the Graham Hancock notion. There's a "level of play" above humans. And the lead-induced departure of four-cat killers via high-speed lead overdose cast me as the level of play one-up from possums.

The Universe is a curiously *nested* series of interlocking structures we can't yet fully understand. Yet can projects like CERN bring us any closer to higher reality than flat landers arguing Higher States?

Honestly don't think so.

A Set of Laws permeates most religious doctrine. Against killing for its own sake. Yet allowed for specific purposes. These Laws, it is suggested, apply to all. Vengeful God on the celestial's plane, to humans on our plane, and possums on theirs.

With this in mind, the one question to have a solid answer to – at check-out time – is "Have you pissed off the Ones on Higher Planes?" For, if you have, it may not go well for you in what follows life.

Just as it hasn't gone well for the cat-eating possums. My vengeance is not yet slaked. But it's getting there. Elaine still misses the cat she was gentling, though.

The data on this "nested laws" part seems cross-cultural and solid although adapted to cultural variances.

The Big Cover-Up – which seems to be inferred but not spoken of directly as a *Commandment* though – is there's a "Get Over It" Law.

- God did smite a good bit. But then got over it.
- Records claim from a smiting meanie He became a good parent.
- I'm doing smiting now myself. Yet I'll get over it, too. Jury is still out on my parenting, but none of mine can walk on water; pretty sure of that.

Sure, as I smite, I still know and appreciate having lived a great Life.

By this Great Unspoken Law, I'll *get over that* one of these days, too.

Should your life also end (spoiler alert: it will), if you find yourself in an extremely warm and foul place loathing everything and existing in pain? Forgive yourself and move to a cooler place. Accept that Grace is a personal thing and that you alone can decide when to *Get Over It*.

We're all understudies in this life. Learning our parts for the Next. This is your Film School Life. Get up every day and shoot the best episode *ever* of your Life Review Film. When your L.R.E comes, the toughest critic is you.

Better hurry, though. You need to pack up (and collect plenty of B-roll) from this life before its own encoded "Get Over It" pull date shows up.

Write when your rich and have filled that suitcase between your ears with your finest treasures.

# # #

Also, by George Ure:

Four times weekly: www.UrbanSurvical.com (1999-present)

Twice weekly: www.Peoplenomics.com (2001-Present)

"The Best Book Ever About Sales"   (2005)

"How to Live on $10,000 a year" (2009, Second Ed. 2013)

"Broken Web: the Coming Collapse of the Internet" (2012)

"11-Steps to a Strategic Life" (with Gaye Levy) (2012)

"DreamOver: An Adventure Novel" (2015)

"Dimensions Next Door: Hacking Space-Time" (2017)

"The Millennial's Missing Manual" (2017)

"Psychocartography: Mapping the Human Mind" (2018)

...*plus* several more in production for 2021 and 2022...